WITH LOVE.

My Experiment with Gravity

REX FINFGELD

Editor: Katie Connolly
Cover Design: Rex Finfgeld
Back cover photo: Eric Wood

Dedication

To my mother and guardian angel. She was the one person who always believed in me and knew I could do something positive in this world! For the first time, I believe it's possible she was right!

Thank you to every single person with whom I have shared, whether a moment in time or a lifetime, this incredible experience we call life!

Contents

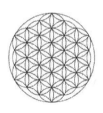

Introduction

In 2011, I had a near-death experience (NDE) that was the most profound, transformational experience of my life! Umm... yeah... I fell out of a tree. I fell 26 feet, landing head first on concrete. This was the catalyst to this most profound moment of being near-death! Now, even though you may realize this book tells the story of my near-death experience and even though you may anticipate that I will describe those moments while on the verge of death...The question paramount on your mind right now isn't "What happened in those moments while near death?" but rather, "What in the world was a grown man doing up in a tree?" Fair enough. We'll get to that.

As a result of that event, I have a second chance to live the life I feel I was always meant to live. The event opened up a chance to fulfill the dreams I had become convinced were out of reach. It was my opportunity to start over in reinventing myself and my life. More and more, I'm doing the things I've always wanted to do and, most importantly, sharing with those I love! I now simply want to do and be all the things I had come to believe were impossible, just as when I was child dreaming about a bright future with endless possibilities!

During the first couple of years after my release from the hospital, instead of referring to the incident as "the fall" or "the accident" (by the way, I have never thought of this experience as an accident), I would often refer to it as "My Experiment with Gravity". The expression became a bit of a running joke among family and friends. It seemed fitting that it be the title of my first book. I have two books to follow in my forthcoming 3-book series, the majority of which has already been written as of this writing. I am calling the series, "The Gravity Series". All of this has been made possible via a traumatic brain injury. Regardless of the physiological processes taking place while near death, there is no denying a dramatic transformation has taken place especially with the incredible openness of my thoughts.

Gravity played an obvious and key role in my falling. There's certainly no disputing that. That unto itself makes it a key piece of this experience. Plus, it's easy to see why I would want to use gravity in the title of the book and the series. However, a few people have commented that gravity has a negative association for them. I've heard comments like, "it pushes/pulls down", "is heavy", "moving through it is difficult", "it's tiring", and have heard it referenced to as "the weight of the world". To many, gravity doesn't seem particularly positive. One person suggested that she didn't like the title referring to gravity's association with "pulling down on you". After all, gravity is at the root of something like falling out of a tree. Nevertheless, this feeling that the series should be "The Gravity Series" persisted within. I could feel something was important about gravity but didn't know what for some time. I have come to realize that there is so much more to gravity than what I think even Einstein or Newton realized. I have come to understand that gravity is truly an amazing and beautiful force of nature! As such, gravity has taken on a much different role for me on this path than being crux of something (or someone) falling from a tree.

Gravity is perhaps the most fundamental force of the universe. But this doesn't just apply to a universal existence but to something more, the multiverse. The reason it doesn't fit into the Theory of Everything (a theory that physicists are seeking to explain the most fundamental properties of the universe in a single simple equation) is because gravity doesn't fit. It is even more fundamental. In addition to gravity, the other three forces largely accepted as the four fundamental forces of the universe are the strong and weak nuclear forces and electromagnetism (light). These three forces seem to work with current theoretical physics models and equations but physicists currently have no idea how gravity fits. Gravity existed before the universal creation and will exist after its demise. It is the most fundamental force from the unified reality to the multi-universal super macrocosm.

I feel deeply that there is something "mindful" about gravity. Perhaps the divine imagination at work in the whole experience? The overall structure of this reality, despite what some scientists suggest (no, this does not go against the Laws of Thermodynamics), is the actions of chaos which are generally only perceived as a negative process of breaking down. While the Laws of Thermodynamics certainly apply in referring to the second law, the law of increasing entropy (the cycle of losing energy and of the process of breaking down), there is nonetheless something completely exacting to this entire process. There is something exacting about the building up and breaking down of this whole universal or even a potential multi-universal existence. Of course, energy is continually changing states (first law). In the context of fractal thinking, even in the perceived chaos there are patterns. Every part of this whole experience from the unified reality to the super macro has an acutely sharp precision of a choir of perfect subatomic, atomic, and molecular harmonies that drive the laws and life process of this universal creation. Without gravity there is no existence, certainly nothing we could experience...

Gravity gives form, function, and shape to everything. Without it, the chemical reactions that give rise to any form of existence as we know it wouldn't happen. Think in terms of energy reacting to gravity, not gravity reacting to energy. Very simply, gravity is the sculptor and the entirety of the prospective multi-universal reality is the clay!

While this book tells the story of my having nearly died, it's also about "coming back" from the verge of death both as the same person I was before but also now as a different person. It's about a person who was a born dreamer who lost sight of those dreams, only to rediscover them. It's about growing and evolving every day on a whole different mindset and path. Simply having a brush with death unto itself can have a deep impact on anyone in getting a true sense of our mortality and the fragile nature of our own life. It can shake one's perspective on what is truly meaningful and important to one's self and life. Even though the material world clearly plays a role in our Earthly life, it's not the only thing. While a key part of the experience, it's arguably not most important thing. There is just so much more! The material world is now just a part of the "fabric of my life" as I am a part of the "fabric".

Time, whether you see it as real, an illusion, or anything else, has become truly precious to me. Life can all be over in an instant no matter who you are or what age. We don't generally get a warning as to when our life will take that drastic turn. Perhaps contracting a terminal illness may offer a range of time for the end of a life. In this case, a person may be paralyzed with fear at the uncertainty of death or even just give up. But for others, a terminal diagnosis evokes drastic changes with a powerful sense of wanting to make the most of the time left. Yes, there is something about being at peace with death that inspires life! Nevertheless, a life can and often does come to a sudden and unexpected end. A person may have a major heart attack, stroke, or a brain aneurism that results in a sudden death. Perhaps it's a car accident, being killed in war, or some unexpected work accident like a fall from building or...a tree. Death can happen at any age, not just to the elderly.

This whole experience has become about so much more than just me. It's not just my about "my experience", but rather the experience itself in expanding into consciousness. I would like to find ways to touch people, inspire them, and bring everyone together in friendship. I hope to do something notable and special to leave a positive mark on the world by the time I do take my last breath. The goal is for this book to be a launching point to that end.

By the time you finish reading this book, I hope you see the potentially endless possibilities in yourself and your life personally. I hope you see the endless possibilities to achieve your dreams or find affirmation in your experience of already doing so. Let's all raise up to living the life of our dreams! I believe the paradigm shift to a higher consciousness worldwide is inevitable. Egotism, war, violence, deceit, and materialism will become obsolete, creating a loving, peaceful, and abundant way of life for all!

1

Dreaming into Life

*"All that we see or seem is but a dream within a dream" -
Edgar Allan Poe*

What are dreams? Is this all a dream, within a dream, within a dream? Simply... yes. This whole reality is infinitely vast, yet the most subtle and delicate experience of the divine. More to the point, it's all the divine imagination manifesting the ultimate dream through infinite experience. It's dreaming in expanding consciousness into the experience through each and every possibility in love, fear, thought, feeling, and idea no matter how fleeting or enduring. But also, divine consciousness is expanding through each duality and relationship of each other and everything. Without the dualities and relationships, there can be no experience and no "you and me". This includes the imagination and dreams of every part of our experience and all of us individually and collectively. All of creation is the collective dream from the imagination of the singular divine being. Every person and every experience is a key part of this divine dream. Dreams are the essence of the deepest foundations of each one of us, connected and interwoven intricately together in the divine imagination in the one singular divine dream.

This book is not as much about near-death experience (NDE) as it is about dreams. Yes, I did have an NDE and we will dive into that. However, it's about the dreams of a small, still innocent child. It's about growing up and like many of us, losing sight of those dreams when assimilating into life as an adult in the "real world". One day, I had a traumatic experience that could have and perhaps should have ended my life. It was the catalyst that opened up a whole new realm of possibilities for me. It was also the rediscovery of the child within and of my lost dreams. As a child I always had the most vivid dreams both waking and sleeping. I had quite the colorful imagination. I had many waking dreams or daydreams. I would dream of the many different amazing possibilities of how my life could unfold. I thought of the potential experience of love I could have, someone with whom I could grow old. Even before I knew what sex was, I would envision the "love of my life". I dreamed of "the one" I would spend a lifetime with and imagined our family. Like many children, I would dream of ways to bring happiness, joy, and love to everyone I touched and to the world. I imagined ways it would happen through writing, film, and music. Now, I find myself dreaming many of my childhood dreams as an adult. Now, I've learned to believe in my dreams. All these many years later, these dreams are now becoming the manifestation of my life. I'm learning to make dreams come true through healing, happiness, joy, and love! The more I am this experience, the more I want to enjoy and spread the love to others.

I now think and dream in ways like I never imagined I could, even as a child. On the one hand I did take on some brain damage, especially with memory. But on the other hand, my mind now works on such a highly visual level that I can make sense of and understand things I never could before. It's the awakening of part of me where the dreams had died. Now I'm not only dreaming in the lucid way I did as a child, but these dreams are taking me on journeys of discovery that continually expand my mind in this human experience. It's not so much that no one else has thought about these things, but prior to the NDE, I certainly never had. This is not to suggest that I didn't have some intellectual or spiritual interests and the ability to have a productive conversation about them, but that was a "drop in the bucket" compared to the flow of information now.

This book is intended to be largely experiential in nature. In this book, I share an overview of my life story and the experience leading up to the NDE. I describe the fall and the subsequent medical issues. The book then transitions into the reality-altering moments while near-death. Since the fall, I have had a lot of time to live with this experience and delve into it. I still ponder it often. Since then, I have had a great many realizations. I see, think, and feel in ways like I never imagined I could. What is, to me, the most important part of the book is sharing some of the epiphanies I've had since this near-death experience. I touch upon the most fundamental parts of our experience - love, spirit, mind, and consciousness. From all of that, I share what I have learned in applying this to our daily lives.

I will also delve into some deep and very subjective topics. Many of these topics cannot yet be proven nor disproven. What I'm about to explain can be explained many different ways depending on the person doing the explaining. But regardless of the choice of words and the many forms of expression, there are often parallels to the ways these deeper subjects can be broken down and explained. I share my own unique experience, perspective, and expression of some of these often deeply esoteric subjects, especially the over-arching topic of dreaming the ultimate dream, the divine dream. The idea is the manifestation of making our dreams come true in our own lives right here on planet Earth.

In the physical world, we can hide truth from each other and even from ourselves. But there is no hiding from the truth of our dreams, whether rooted in the material or something often less immediately tangible like love. They are the pure reflection of who and what we truly are as well as the path in life we walk. Dreaming is a potent form of manifestation of the physical reality and what we experience in our lives. It is a truth that is revealed as what is inside you in that moment regarding intention. Intentions manifest thoughts, thoughts manifest dreams, dreams manifest this reality. But then, even the physical reality is a form of dream unto itself. It can be a nightmare, it can be beautifully fulfilling, or many things in between. What do you dream about? As Dennis DeYoung of the rock group, Styx, said as he introduced the song "Come Sail Away" on the live album called "Caught in the Act"… "Dreams do come true!" In thinking about dreams, I stay focused on reaching out and continuing to co-create a life I feel we all were always meant to have in a loving, compassionate reality with many wonderful, intelligent, and talented people working together for a peaceful world! The more the merrier…

2

A Brief Evolution of my Dreams

What is a dream to you? Do you dream? What do you dream about? Are you living your dreams or any part of them? What is that motivates and inspires you?

I was quite the dreamer as a child. I loved to fantasize and I loved to dream. Dreaming was always an important part of me and my personal well-being. I had some truly fantastic dreams as well as some rather scary ones. I was always deeply fascinated with the dreams we experience whether sleeping or awake. Even as just a little child, I would spend hours contemplating my dreams in addition to the time experiencing the dreams. I always believed I learned from my dreams. I found them so much fun! My dreams were so vivid that I remember believing that what I dreamed was just as real as what I experienced while being awake. This included my nightmares and I had many. For me as a child, the line between dreaming and being awake was rather blurred. There were times I would realize I was dreaming and find myself being able to control it. Now I realize I was lucid dreaming. The first thing I did when I had my first lucid dream was fly. I flew right out into space. I woke up at that point. I would sometimes, upon realizing I was dreaming, go into the ocean. I would breathe under water like it was some kind of heavy air. Funny, even now I can remember the sensation of it. There were times when I would want to talk about it, but the conversation didn't often go very far. No one was particularly interested. Needless to say, I was incredibly fascinated with dreams and dreaming!

It wasn't just about the dreams I had while sleeping. I was also ever the consummate daydreamer. I thoroughly enjoyed and was perfectly comfortable living in my dreams. I was always a big fan of "Ralph Phillips" from the Looney Tunes cartoons. He was quite the daydreamer. He had many epic adventures in his dreams and, as a result, was often in trouble with his teacher! There were only a few cartoons that featured him but one where he was the main character was one of my favorites! I was a lot like him as a kid. I often neglected schoolwork or a lesson being taught by the teacher in favor of my daydreams. Yes, I was often in trouble with my teachers. If I was focused on my daydreams, that means I clearly wasn't listening to the teacher or doing my work. So, I would miss the lesson and worse, my schoolwork would be late, sometimes very late. Worse still, sometimes the schoolwork just didn't get done. I was fortunate not to have been held back a grade.

My 5th grade year had to be the worst and the closest I came to being held back a grade. My teacher would completely "lose his mind" when I wasn't listening or didn't get my work done. I can't begin to remember how many times he would yell at me at the top of his lungs in front of the class. He really went out of his way to make an example of me. The sad thing is that, as a teaching professional for 5th graders, I think he genuinely hated me. He would get so angry! I'm talking full-on red-faced angry! I certainly wasn't motivated to be there. I hated him and school at that point.

Once during the school year, my mother was informed by this teacher that I wasn't doing well in class. She sat me down and had a nice talk with me. She always believed I was a smart kid and she reminded me of that. As a promise to my mom, I decided I would do my work in class. I had a day where not only did I do my work, but I was the first to finish. When I turned in my work, the teacher very sarcastically said something to the effect of, "If I could get everyone's attention, please. For once, Rex actually did his work. Now let's see how he did, shall we?" He proceeded to grade my paper in front of the class making sort of "play-by-play" comments aloud as he went through it. He would act shocked as I got each part of assignment correct. When it turned out I did the whole assignment correctly, he went on with the class, "We should really celebrate this moment. He actually did the work and actually did it right. Let's all give him a round of applause, shall we?!" The class awkwardly clapped. My classmates were clearly uncomfortable. I remember in my kid-mind thinking that while he came across as overly nice, there was an "icky" feeling about that whole experience. When I told my mother what happened, she about "went through the roof"! She was pissed! She went to the school the next day and "had a little chat" with the teacher. I know it didn't go well for him. From then on, he was at least cordial to me. He certainly didn't yell anymore. That was definitely the closest I came to being held back a grade. He felt strongly that I wouldn't ready for the 6th grade.

My grades were never great but during my 5th grade year they were by far the worst. My elementary school didn't use letter grades. It was a three-grade system used in quite few categories in addition to the main subject grades. They used a "+" sign for a top grade, a triangle basically saying passable but could use some improvement, and the letter "N" reflecting the lowest mark saying the work in below average. Even though my report cards that year routinely had lots of "N's", he passed me. Looking back, I think that teacher really didn't want to deal with me or my mom for another year.

As a child, I had so many dreams both sleeping and waking. They always felt so clear, vivid, and strong...like I was actually living them. I often had recurring dreams in my sleep. There were some that would go on for years. Perhaps the most perplexing, profound, and long-lasting of my recurring dreams was about a huge, ancient black dragon and a particular land. There was a dragon sleeping beneath a huge castle in a beautiful green mountainous region. It was like something out of the "Lord of the Rings" movie. I felt that this dragon had been sleeping for hundreds if not thousands of years. He was beyond huge. He was utterly enormous! I could feel his sheer incredible power with every snoring breath. I knew he was going to wake up, but I didn't know when. I was frightened of this possibility! I wanted so bad to just leave and get away, but I just couldn't. I would make an effort to escape this land, sometimes even just the castle, and get as far away from the dragon as possible, but I found myself going in circles. I couldn't get far enough not to feel him.

When the dreams began, I was elementary aged. Everything was so clear in the dream. I can recall neighboring towns at various locations around the castle and this town. I'm not sure how to estimate the populations but there were fair-sized populations of people in these towns. The earliest of these dreams took place in one or several of the towns in this land. It was generally an isolated area. The strange thing was that, despite this dragon, none of the people ever seemed worried. They could never understand why I would want to leave. Yet they were always most helpful. I could usually see the castle somewhere off in the distance. I always felt like I needed to find something but had no idea what. It felt like there were variations of a story in the scope of a single dream, but that there was an overarching ongoing story with the repetition of these dreams over the years.

As I got older, I continued having the dreams. I finally decided to stop trying to leave this land and/or castle. The fear was starting to subside. I felt a strong familiarity with the elements of the dream. There were times when the dreams were almost enjoyable. The people in these dreams were always supportive and caring. There were even some recurring "characters". Every so often, I would get a surge of fear that the dragon was getting ever closer to waking up. I still had no idea what would happen when he did. I thought it would be something horrible. But I was accepting that I would eventually have to deal with the ramifications of whatever that was going to be.

The overarching dream evolved to where there was sometimes the element of finding and rescuing someone like a princess. She was my princess or rather my angel. The reason or point of trying to find her wasn't clear to me but I felt that although I had never seen her, I knew her somehow. For years I simply couldn't find her. That was just part of the mystery because I certainly didn't know why I was in a land I couldn't leave. But this angel was somehow connected to me and I felt she needed me. I would be trying to get to her to save her but I wouldn't be able to find her. I assumed that I had to do it before the dragon woke up. The fear of the dragon's awakening was getting stronger again. Eventually, the dream evolved to me being only in the castle. I could hear the slow rumbling from the breath of the sleeping dragon.

As the dream continued to progress, I found myself residing in the castle. The dream continued to evolve to where I realized the castle was mine. The handful of people I encountered were subjects of the castle somehow. While there, I could sometimes smell a stench of burnt rotting flesh. Once again, I was feeling like I wanted to leave. But now I was torn because I could feel this angel also in the castle and I couldn't find her. I would comb the castle looking for her, so we could leave together. I just couldn't leave her! I was paralyzed with fear trying to find figure out what was happening while still wanting to find my way out. I felt like the dragon would kill me if he found me there. What would he do to the angel if he found her?

This whole experience felt so lucid and real as I was feeling lost and confused. While I moved throughout the castle it was surprisingly empty yet perfectly clean. I did encounter a few people throughout multiple dreams while in the castle as mentioned. Some of the memory has faded but I believe there was a guardsman, two ladies who may have been seamstresses, and a few others whose roles are a bit fuzzy. They were still always friendly and always seemed to want to help me.

Eventually the dream kept taking me to the verge of finding the angel and together finding our way out of the castle. At times, it felt as if I had found her and we were together yet somehow, she was always just out of reach. Many of the images of her are spotty and fleeting, especially now.

There were some basic variations of this dream as it progressed over the years well into adulthood, but it was always with the same basic theme. Eventually, the fear and anticipation began to wane as I was finding myself becoming at peace with whatever was to happen. The dragon finally had awakened. I was 44 years old at the time, having just had the NDE. It was such a great relief. I felt a sense of being somehow liberated.

I realized that the dragon was a representation of the true me. Especially now, it has become clear that I had been running from myself, or rather my true self. We all have a strength and power that comes as part of the discovery of one's true self and true path. It takes strength and power to walk such a path. I feared my own strength and power. I feared my own potential. Even more, I feared failing to achieve it. As ridiculous as it sounds, it was almost easier to hold back, mired in all of my negative patterns, and not bother. That way it becomes easier to accept when things just don't work out. It was easier to say "hey, I tried" or "that's just life". It was a familiar pattern to me. After all, who the heck was I to live in light and in so doing accomplish positive things, leaving a positive mark on the world, love and be loved, and be abundant? My perception was that I was undeserving of such a position in life and the responsibility that comes with it. However, this was a time when I was at the core beginnings of starting to move toward my highest life path in my personal quest for self-discovery. As I struggled with my past, I feared what was really inside of me. Also, in feeling undeserving, I often held myself back and this left me feeling weak and powerless.

I'm still not yet completely clear what the angel represents. I do have an idea. Perhaps she is a reflection of my own feminine nature. After all, the truth is all of us has both sexes within us no matter how masculine or feminine one may appear. Maybe she was a spiritual guide (I've since discovered an affinity for the angel Jophiel). The angel could be a reflection or a karmic correlation of a prospective special love in my life. Maybe she is all of this and more. The more I learn about my dreams the more I see multiple or overlapping stories and messages.

In my martial art of Kun Tao Silat, each movement in our forms has multiple applications. In other words, there are multiple interpretations and meanings for every move. I've realized dreams can work much in the same way. It's not just one meaning per dream. There may well be and likely are multiple meanings. I'm seeing more and more how my dreams and my thoughts interconnect and overlap. I can see the different levels of the meanings and connections in the various parts of my life. If you pay attention, you'll notice similar connections and meanings unique to your life within your dreams both waking and sleeping.

I had some fun fantasies with my daydreams. My favorite is a fantasy that many kids have - being in a band that became internationally successful. I actually named this fantasy, which I didn't often do. I affectionately referred to this fantasy as "Rock band Rex". In this fantasy, I was a songwriter, singer, and a virtuoso guitar player. I also played piano/keyboards and some drums. The band was a fusion of Rock, Soul/dance, and underground Electronica. It was definitely "Alternative" for the time. I would pick songs from a handful of bands I liked that were somewhat obscure but that seemed to go together. This gave the fantasy a dose of reality. The songs often reflected where I was at a given point in my life. As music often does, they sometimes reflected my pain. But also, some songs were positive, uplifting, and enduring. I liked the idea of emoting feeling. For much of my life, especially as a young man, I had some nice, and loud, stereo systems. I would "rock out" to select songs as the tracks this special band I was in would perform. In my fantasy, we had our hits and we played big concerts all over the world. Eventually the members had their own projects but would come back together to write and record a new album. However, I could never settle on a single name. Yes, it was quite the elaborate fantasy and went on for many years, just like many of my fantasies. This was quite the positive way to vent so many of the negative feelings of those times in my life. It was also a form of escapism from being unhappy in life and in an unhappy world. I often wished I could be somewhere or someone else, living a different life. It was nice not only to feel successful but to feel that I was genuinely good at something, especially something that I could share with almost everybody. I've always liked connecting with people through music.

Especially when I was a teenager, I would imagine living lives as someone or something completely different from me. I imagined any number of people but also animals and even alien forms of life. I never wanted to be a specific past or present human being other than myself, so anyone or any likeness I would fantasize about would be totally imaginary in still being me. I would be this person who, in my mind, would be better than me in getting better grades, being a better athlete, being thin, and being well liked, mainly by girls. I would sometimes imagine living this type of life in various forms with different storylines. I even imagined being different animals such as an eagle, tiger, and gorilla, among others. I liked to imagine the things they could do and their lives as animals. I sometimes dreamed of many different lives on different worlds as beings that were very sophisticated and intellectually advanced. These beings would naturally have to be far more evolved than humans. I sometimes felt confined and limited in my body. Even then, I dreamed of being in a place of higher consciousness even though I didn't understand it quite in that context. I did dream of a life experience of being wise and knowledgeable, even universally vast. I dreamed of traveling the universe at will. In so doing, I would have breathtaking experiences witnessing the birth and death of planets, stars, and entire galaxies and so much more. I would travel into the heart of the most massive black holes. I would imagine traversing dimensions. In this way, I had a sense that I could be anything and that anything was possible, even if not here in this world.

I often dreamed about my life as an adult. Even as a young adult I would imagine future possibilities. I created different scenarios of an amazing and successful life. I wasn't always crazy about being a kid while being a kid. I looked forward to growing up. Because money was always tight growing up post-divorce, a big part of these fantasies included being a millionaire. Sometimes, the fantasy would blow up to being a billionaire. I believed such things were possible.

I would dream about being successful in various ways. An obvious one, as for many boys, is as an athlete. I imagined myself generally as a baseball, football player, and sometimes a motocross racer (common boyhood dream growing up in Michigan). As a baseball player, I was a catcher and hit the clean-up spot at 4th in the batting order. As a football player, I liked defense. I often pictured being an inside linebacker because I liked the hitting. I considered, too, if had gotten big enough, maybe defensive tackle. Of course, I would be a sack artist in getting to the quarterback and making the big play. I also felt I could be a great actor with the right training and experience. I would imagine movies I would be in. Some would be suspense thrillers, others cool sci-fi films, and some would be deeply romantic. I imagined I could sing and dance. I pondered starring in a modern-day musical. This fantasy would eventually give way to being a filmmaker and an author. I dreamed of writing a book and screenplay of my own vampire story. I also imagined my version of a high-tech sci-fi movie. I was a serious fantasy role-player. A fantasy movie or book wouldn't be out of the question either. I primarily played "Dungeons and Dragons". I played a few others like "Gamma World", a post-apocalyptic era game, and "Traveller", a game set in a "Star Trek" or "Star Wars" type of environment. There was also a great game set in the old west called "Boot Hill". I also played "Vampire the Masquerade". I was so inspired by the idea of role-playing games that I created my own gaming system designed to be used in any era set by the game master or the story-teller. I had the opportunity to play a bit with my brother and some friends and they generally liked it. I was often the dungeon or game master or rather the story teller. I felt some of the many adventures my friends and I shared would make great books or movies one day. I sometimes liked to imagine being a successful businessman. I would have homes all over the world. I would have large properties in many locations. I mostly imagined using these properties as places I could do more outdoor activities like hiking, motorcycling, snowmobiling, scuba diving, or just staring at the stars in a beautiful locale. I even imagined having my own "mini-Keck" type of telescope on a piece of property on the western slope of Colorado. I've always loved losing myself in the stars. I loved to imagine what was possibly out there. In another fantasy, I would be a world leader with scenarios in different parts of the world. I even imagined a united Europe. No matter where I was, I would help usher in ages of prosperity. I always believed the resources exist here on Earth to care for everyone. I imagined mediating the end of wars and bringing people from all over the world together. But no matter what the fantasy was, I wanted to bring something positive and awesome to the world. I've always wanted to make people feel good and smile.

I imagined having children. I would picture different numbers up to three. I imagined what they may look like, what they may do, and the people they would become. I imagined both sons and daughters. I dreamed about a tight-knit family. Even though there would be the ups and downs that all families experienced, my wife and I led by example. We would always persevere and work things out. We let the kids be kids but made sure to help them find their talents and nurture them. As a late bloomer myself, and knowing this when I was a kid, I would picture one or more of my children being the "odd ball" kid, the one that was different and needed time to find him or herself. I tried to be as realistic as I could as far as such a fantasy goes. In watching many of my friends' kids grow up, I know things can turn out quite differently than thought possible but still turn out well.

As a lifelong romantic, the biggest thing I loved to fantasize about was meeting the love of my life. She was to be my lover and best friend. Cue the orchestra...I would imagine being married and growing old with that someone special. I did often wonder who she could be and what she might be like. I'm not sure many young boys have this fantasy. For me, I couldn't wait to have the experience of the love of a woman. I didn't want to wait until I was older. I thought the sooner my life partner and I connected, the more time we would have together. That was the one thing I wanted more than anything, even as a boy! Of course, boys have their sexual fantasies, which I did. I certainly imagined making love to this woman. I often imagined veritable adventures in making passionately beautiful love with my beloved girlfriend/wife in many potentially romantic places around the world! I would also think about being romantic and intimate spending a day and/or night in various places, from Prague in the summertime admiring the ancient architecture, catching the London Symphony at the Barbican Centre, experiencing the Shaolin Monks in northern China, traveling to pyramids of the Mayans and the Egyptians, seeing Victoria Falls in southern Africa, and clubbing in LA or Ibiza. Computers didn't start making their way into households until I was in high school, so I read encyclopedias to fuel my fantasies. I imagined sitting under a full moon on a California beach staring at the moon and stars while sharing our deepest and most intimate secrets. Though even a small child, I imagined a closeness with women. Of course, I didn't fully understand these feelings but I knew I yearned for them. As a teenager, I wanted affection more than sex (though not by much...after all, I was still an adolescent boy). Virtually every fantasy or dream I had of different versions of my adult life, I always envisioned it with my "forever love".

I would even daydream about what it would be like to be old. I imagined my children all grown up with children of their own. I would run many of these fantasies through the course of a whole life to the point of dying. Fantasies like this helped to alleviate my fear of death as I was getting into my teenage years. Though I still had no real concept of being dead, how I lived my life started to become important. I wanted to be someone my mother could be proud of. I wanted to be someone who would leave a positive mark on the world.

I thought about being at the end of my life and how I would feel looking back at my life on the proverbial death bed. I would envision being able to look back at an amazing fulfilling life, a life I could be happy with, especially with that certain special someone. I wanted to look back at a life with the ultimate experience of love. Of course, a life partner is paramount to that experience, but I pictured an experience of love that was somehow worldwide. This love was shared by many people partly from the positive impact I imagined I might have from whatever work I ended up doing and the life I dreamed of living! Of course, considering the different dreams I had, there was long list of possibilities!

I imagined what it would be like at that moment of dying. How might it happen? Would I be young, middle aged, or elderly? I always imagined, as I think most do, that I would be quite elderly when I died. Would it be a fast death like a car accident or a massive heart attack? Would it be something drawn out like cancer? Would I die in my sleep? Would I die in the arms of the one I love? There was something that had resonated about that. However, I thought it would be better for my spouse if she passed first. That way she wouldn't have to live through my passing. But at the same time, I certainly wouldn't have wanted to shorten her life especially if she should be younger than me. I was never sure what age I would imagine my wife to be. I did have fantasies imagining my wife as being older, younger, or the same age, depending on the particular fantasy.

One movie deeply moved me as a kid. I remember when I saw "The World According to Garp". This may be a partial spoiler alert so maybe skip to the next paragraph if you haven't seen the movie or read the book. But here we go...It's one of my personal favorite movies. The main character, T.S.

Garp, played by Robin Williams, always dreamed about flying. Garp was quite the dreamer too. But he never got the chance to fly in his life. At the end, Garp gets shot. The wound is fatal and he is dying. In an attempt to save his life, he is taken away on a helicopter to be transported to a hospital. He is accompanied by his wife Helen, played by Mary Beth Hurt. She is holding Garp's hand and looking tearfully into his eyes knowing he is about to die. He says to her to "Remember everything." She says, "Yes, my love." He looks out of the helicopter where he has a view of the beautiful green landscape below and says, "I'm flying, Helen," and she says, "Yes, my love." She then embraced him as he went into his final sleep dying in her arms. While very sad, it was just so beautiful! Not that I want to go out like Garp, but leaving this world in the arms of the one you love would be the ultimate way to go! Dying in one's sleep is certainly ideal but even if I was in pain, I would rather die in the arms of someone I love. However, I would actually think about it both ways. If I am to be the one to hold my love at her time of passing, I would want to make it as loving and precious a moment as possible for her to leave the world! Yes, this is what I was dreaming about as a boy and young man. I think I was about 15 or 16 when I saw first saw "The World According to Garp". For the first time, it made me think a lot about my life and how I wanted to leave it.

With death, like love, one never knows for sure how or when it will happen. Love and death often have no apparent rhyme or reason. We don't generally get a conscious choice of when either is going to happen. It just does. There is often no sense of timing or a "rhyme or reason" for either one. Sometimes they happen at the seemingly most inopportune moments or at the most perfect of moments.

**

When I was 8 years old, I had my first experience with the death of someone close. My grandfather on my father's side had already passed away. I did love him. He was good to my brother and me. But because he was elderly and we only saw him from time to time, it wasn't the same as someone passing who you see almost every day, and it isn't the same as when someone who is only 11 years old dies. His name was Jeff. He was often called "Jeffy". He was my first true best friend!

     We met when I was 5 and we instantly became best friends. My family had just moved into a new house and Jeff was one of the first people I met. He lived a couple doors up and across the street. We pretty much just started playing and being kids. Yes, three years isn't that long in the span of a whole life, but at 8 years old that was almost half of my young life. I felt we knew each other forever. I couldn't imagine life without Jeffy. We both had many of the same interests especially when we played "make believe". We were both fans of "Lost in Space" and "Star Trek". Because he was older, he would always be Professor John Robinson, the father of the family in space and captain of the spaceship, "The Jupiter 2". I would always be Major Don West, John Robinson's right-hand man. In "Star Trek", he was Captain James T. Kirk and I was Mr. Spock. The monkey bars in his backyard doubled as the "Jupiter 2" and the "Enterprise". The adventures we would have! We both had quite the active imaginations! So these adventures were lots of fun! It's been so long that I can't remember a specific story line, but we had many. Nonetheless, we seriously threw ourselves into our "make believe" time! In those years, I think we actually only got mad at each other once, maybe twice. Everything always seemed to flow so easily with us. He was a great friend indeed! To this day, I can still hear his laugh and see his face perfectly clearly.

     I remember that there were a couple of days where I wasn't allowed to see him because he was sick. Then I was told that he had been taken to the hospital but he should be ok. But then I was told that Jeffy had died. It was most unexpected for me and I believe for everyone. I loved him so much! We had a rather nice, fun friendship! He was such a sweet kid! When he died, my parents did their best to explain it to me. They weren't religious but told me about Heaven. I wanted to believe he was really going to Heaven!

I didn't have any understanding of death or what it was. Of course, very few do. My mother had explained it to me like going to sleep only you never wake up. I remember asking her, "If death is the final sleep, is he dreaming?" She said, "He is having the happiest dreams in Heaven!" I asked, "If that's true, are dreams real?" I became almost consumed with thinking about death and what it was. I wanted to imagine the dreams that Jeff was having. I imagined myself dead. I would picture what it would be like to exist without the physical body. I thought about what it would be like in a state of always dreaming. The best I could do is compare it to when I was asleep. When I thought of sleep, I always thought of dreaming because of my rather vivid dreams. But exactly what was Jeff dreaming about? Was it Heaven, God, or maybe angels? Was it loved ones? Was it something altogether different? I imagined it had to be something amazing because Jeff was a genuinely good person.

Right after he died, people were talking about having a funeral for Jeff. Naturally, I had no idea what that meant. My mother very nicely explained it to me. It was to be open casket. She explained that as well. I couldn't imagine bearing witness to seeing my best friend being dead. Initially my parents didn't think it would be a good idea if I went. But I bugged them relentlessly to let me go. I felt strongly that I had to be there! They eventually gave in and I could go the funeral.

When we got to the funeral home, I recall being surprised by how nice it was. The first thing I noticed, however, was the smell. I've never smelt anything like it and it was very distinct. Perhaps it was the formaldehyde or something like it used in preparing the body to be shown, but it smelled like death to me. I remember the smell, especially since I've been to open casket funerals since. Each time I noticed a similar scent. Strangely it doesn't make me uncomfortable. If anything, despite my sadness, I always feel a sense of comfort. In a way, it wasn't pleasant but at the same time it wasn't bad per se. It was somehow ok.

When we went into the viewing room, there were many people there, both family and friends. I was pretty blown away when I saw Jeff in the casket. He did look like he was sleeping. He was so still and peaceful. Initially I couldn't help but hope he would wake up right there and we could go off and play. I asked my mom if I could go pray by Jeffy. I walked up next him in his casket and knelt beside him with my hands together in prayer. Tears were streaming down my face. I told him, "I couldn't wait to see him in Heaven someday!" and that "I hoped he was having happy dreams in Heaven!"

Yes, I was always the avid dreamer whether sleeping or waking, with a propensity for constant daydreaming. It was a big distraction to my life and sometimes was even bigger than my life. Many of these dreams stayed with me into my early adulthood. I accept that dreams were a form of escapism, yet they weren't entirely about escaping. I genuinely loved being in my mind and my dreams. With a thought, I could be anyone or anything anywhere I wanted. I loved exploring in my imagination!

I so wanted to believe that the whole world and all people were basically good, especially as an elementary school aged child. I wanted to believe that people generally watched out for each other and did right by one another, especially adults. I wanted to believe that everything always works out in a positive way. I wanted to believe that adults were always trustworthy. I wanted to believe that they were always going to do the honest thing. As a child, I could see that children weren't always nice to each other. I believed that adults were to set an example for children in how to treat one another. It always seemed that adults were often preaching the "be nice, be honest, and be good" type of mindset. I wanted to believe all of that and did my best to carry that out as a kid.

I didn't have much interest in the news. But the TV I did watch always had a happy ending, with everyone eventually doing the right thing. I would watch shows like "Happy Days", "Good Times", or even something like "Emergency" or "Adam 12". The story lines of those shows typically ended on a positive note. In the end, everything always worked out and everybody was happy.

When I would hear of the difficulties of the world or other people's lives, I didn't want to believe it. If I did accept such a hardship I wanted to believe it would always be positive in the end with all involved having the best of intentions. I remember I had befriended a kid named Danny a few houses down from mine. Both of his birth parents had divorced and remarried. He was living with his birth mother and step dad, Eleanor and Rich. He would see his birth father on the weekends. That was a pretty regular routine for him and his family. He also had two step sisters. I think I was in the 4th grade when he moved to the neighborhood. It was the 70's so I'm sure there was more divorce around me than I was aware of. I had heard of it happening fairly often as divorce was on the rise back then. But this kid was the first friend I was close to who had been through divorce. In many ways, this was much like an "ABC Afternoon Special" where the parties involved acted responsibly and at the end there would be a positive life lesson. My friend and his stepdad cared about each other, though they argued often. I remember the stepdad was a good guy. He was always nice to all the kids in our neighborhood.

However, that was probably the first time I ever heard a kid talking back to an adult. I could never imagine talking back to my parents. Danny saw his Dad on weekends. As I recall I don't think his Dad ever missed any visitation time. As far as someone having to go through something like a divorce, this was as ideal of a situation as one could hope. As a kid, this was how I thought everybody acted when dealing with some form of adversity. I always thought everything would always be ok.

**

I was generally a happy kid at least up until the 6th grade (I'll get into that later), or perhaps 5th given the experience with my teacher. I can only recall a handful of moments where I did something that wasn't particularly positive or nice especially as a young child. But overall, I was a nice kid who tended to like everybody and just wanted to be liked. It was always my fondest wish to have fun and be friends with everyone!

I wanted to believe the world was place where dreams could and would come true for anyone and everyone. I wanted so much to believe in magic and that love as the most powerful magic was the driving force to life and the Earth. I believed that the wonderfully unimaginable was possible. I held on to those ideals far longer than most kids my age, including believing in Santa Claus. I was one of the last kids that I grew up with to find that out or, more to the point, perhaps accept that truth. I cried my eyes out! That was perhaps the first moment my romantic perceptions of the world and life started to crumble. After all, what kind of a world were we living in for there to be no Santa Claus?

During the elementary years of my childhood, I had idealized and romanticized life. I believed in the good of everyone. I had idealized America and to an extent Christianity.

Christianity was the only religion that I had any level of exposure to in my life at that time. It didn't occur to me as a child that others, even in America, would believe differently. For that matter it didn't occur to me that Christianity had some many different versions or rather denominations with so many different and conflicting beliefs. Throughout this time, I believed in God and that God was loving and good. I believed in Jesus, though I didn't exactly understand what the idea of the crucifixion was. I mean I knew the belief was that he died on the cross for our sins. But during that period in my life, I didn't fully grasp the concept of a sin. I recall sometimes going to church and feeling like, though we didn't go often, that was what we were supposed to believe. During my later elementary years, I started to see that different people have different beliefs as I started to hear some bits and pieces about it. It was mostly through occasionally paying attention to the news when it was on TV, maybe catching a documentary, or overhearing a conversation between adults. In the 6th grade, my teacher presented a lesson on what he considered the five major religions of the world. That included Christianity, Judaism, Islam, Hinduism, and Buddhism. I found it interesting but like many who believe in Christianity, I felt that other religions were wrong or just made no sense. They felt very foreign to me despite the fact that each of these religions is practiced in America.

By the 6th grade, despite the new insights into different religions, I was beginning to struggle with ideas of God. I eventually came to see the problems of the world. I started to pay a bit more attention to the news and people around me. I was noticing more of the hardships. It didn't help that the US, especially Michigan, was in a recession. I was seeing more of the not-so-nice things people would do to each other, my mother, and sometimes to me. If there was a God, I thought he must not think much of us. It seemed that much of the world was completely forgotten or forsaken. I started to see TV programming that showed starving children and people being beat up and shot. Like many, I couldn't imagine how a loving God could allow such horrible and tragic things to happen to so many people all over the world.

I was far less sure about any religion at that point and many of the people that practiced it. I didn't notice much difference between people who were religious or those who weren't. People who were religious weren't any nicer or any more honest than those who were non-religious. That was a time when I started to realize that "people are people" with some good and some bad no matter what walk of life they come from. I started having a harder time seeing the point in religion. I felt instead that it was at the root of many of the world's problems.

My mother, though not seriously religious, considered herself Episcopalian. We attended church from time to time but almost always on Christmas Eve. She loved the Christmas service. However, my mother was always open to different philosophies and ideas which opened the door for me to at least have some exposure. She largely explored astrology, Fot Choy, Eckankar, and other areas of the occult. She was generally rather open-minded but astrology was of particular interest for her. I developed some curiosity for certain aspects of the occult getting into my teenage years. Like my mom, I developed an interest in astrology but I was also contemplating magical systems like Wicca. My mom had some friends that were into different spiritual practices. With respect to astrology, Tarot, or something like Palmistry, I always had a fascination for understanding the nature of people. During this time, I came to understand that what you see is not necessarily what you get in a person. I found some connections with astrology as I observed certain consistencies with people that matched what the astrology books were saying on the basic traits and qualities of each sign. The idea that the day and time one was born corresponded with certain celestial alignments made some sense to me. Plus, it was somewhat surprising to me the amount of detail there is to the practice when you delve deeply in to it. It's quite a task to create and interpret a "natal chart", especially before computers. It covers many things and can be read on the scale of a person's full life. Most who used it believed in its accuracy. My mother had a couple of friends who used it to essentially help chart a life path. As I observed people's personalities, including my own, I noticed certain consistencies, although I didn't buy in entirely as I noticed some inconsistencies too. But in fairness my understanding of something as in depth as a natal chart was mostly beyond me. Although overall it is still a very esoterically-based spiritual system, it seemed to have at least something I could "put my finger on". A big reason for this interest is that I've always been a "student" of human nature and understanding. Largely because of my mother and some of her friends, I had an opportunity to explore some different ideas and philosophies.

Regarding Christianity, I didn't know what to think about Jesus or, for that matter, the Buddha, Muhammad, or any such prophetic figure. I will say, however, I could never wrap my mind around the idea that when you die, that there was nothing else. In spite of my doubts, I always felt there was something more than this life. But I didn't even begin to have a thought as what that might be.

While I did have some "hard to explain" experiences, I still had a difficulty perceiving beyond the five senses. I started to have a fascination for psychic phenomena and ghosts. Even with my interest in things supernatural, I wanted to believe but was not quite able to make that "leap of faith" to something beyond the physical senses and unprovable. I did have "supernatural" experiences that were arguably within the realm of the physical senses. In other words, I saw something unexplainable with my eyes and even felt something physically. Three different experiences involved seeing ghosts or spirits. I also had some rather powerful, even prophetic, dreams.

The first "supernatural" experience happened shortly after Jeff died. Sometime shortly thereafter, I was sleeping in the top bunk of my bunkbed. I'm not sure exactly what woke me up but in the dark I saw a softly glowing image of a boy crouched down at the foot of my bed. Being in the top bunk there wasn't a lot of room from my bed to the ceiling. The image was distinct but still somehow obscured. I couldn't be sure who it was. This hazy image felt friendly. My first impulse was it was Jeffy. So, I spoke to him. The boy smiled and slowly faded away. It was a very peaceful experience. I cried as I missed him so much and wished that he would come back. I certainly couldn't go back to sleep after that. Of course, I had to learn the hard lesson that death was final. I never saw that spirit again. It was like a sort of goodbye while letting me know that he was well.

The second time was most frightening for me! In hindsight, it bore the feeling of some sort of very dark fully sentient being. Some may refer to this as a demon. I was having a horrible nightmare that a demon was pursuing me in a dark old mansion. However, it was in the form of an excruciatingly vile old man. It was like something out of "Poltergeist" but worse. It was the scariest horror movie you can imagine! This "man" was so incredibly and completely angry! I knew it wasn't just an old man as he was very strong in the dream and had something penetratingly dark in his eyes. I kept trying to run but to not much avail. It seemed the faster I tried to move the more resistance I got. It was like running while under water but there was no water in the dream. No matter where I went, this creature was right there, taunting me like it knew it had me where it wanted me. At some point, I ended up in my bedroom in the dream. Somehow, I, while still sleeping, was standing in front of my bedroom closet, holding the doors closed with all my might as I cried out for my parents. That's when I woke up. The closet was next to my bed, this time a simple twin bed. When I awoke, I realized I had jumped out of my bed while desperately pushing against the closed closet doors with my arms, yelling "Mom, Dad... Help!!" I could still feel "it" banging against the closet doors and trying to push the doors open. I continued to yell. When my parents came in, the banging stopped. Both closet doors were off their hinges but pushed out toward me. One door was bent across the middle. Yes, it's easy to write this off as a dream but both doors were off their hinges, pushed into the room with a notable outward dent. It is highly unlikely that considering my proximity to the door, the fact that I was holding the doors with palms of my hands, and the fact that I was about 10 years old, I could have done this myself. I can't deny that there is plenty of room for speculation. After all, I was a young kid with a very active imagination. Plus, it was a long time ago. But given the complete clarity of the dream even all these years later including the banging on the closet door, I now must contend that something extraordinary happened.

The third time was quite bizarre. I'm still not sure what to make of it. This was a couple of years later. It was a weekend morning. I had woken up and was listening to music but was still lying in bed. I rolled over and standing in front of my bedroom door was a short stocky man. He was barefoot and dressed in a bright orange robe with yellow symbols all around it. Unfortunately, I don't recall what the symbols were or looked like. He was very fair skinned and had long curly, bushy blond hair. I wasn't afraid as I spoke to him. I said, "Hello, why are you here?" He just looked at me relatively straight faced but didn't respond. Gradually he disappeared into thin air. Again, I realize there's lots of room for speculation but the clarity of the memory and the impact it had was undeniable regardless of how one chooses to rationalize it. Unfortunately, I don't have a "logical" explanation for this or the previous "ghost" stories. All I can say is that they left an indelible impression on me. I even had an experience of seeing a UFO. Once again, I don't have a logical explanation for this and I am not presuming to know exactly what it was. I'm not specifically saying it came from outer space but I will say it is highly unlikely this was a human-made craft, especially at that time. This would have been in the mid-to-late 70's in the early morning as I was walking from my bedroom to the bathroom. We had a set of glass doors that looked out to a swimming pool we had back then, when my parents were married. I saw a small round reddish light that sort of twinkled. It seemed to be rather far away, or perhaps it was just small. I can't be sure about that. It was sitting still, hovering in the air. I first thought it was a light from a helicopter but it didn't quite look like any lights on any helicopters I had seen before. I continued to watch it. After about a minute or so, it moved. It rather instantaneously moved upward then what appeared to be away. It maneuvered very quickly and moved at such a speed that this craft, or whatever it was, had to be a technology beyond anything on Earth. I do recall there were other people on the local news who reported seeing it. It was said to be a weather balloon. Maybe it wasn't extraterrestrial but there was no way this was a weather balloon. A weather balloon doesn't make sharp abrupt movements or turns. They are rather slow moving. But because no one at the time took it seriously, I had no frame of reference with respect to this experience. There was no one to talk to about this. I essentially put this episode out of my mind until recently.

**

My younger brother Scott and I were raised primarily by my mother. When my parents were married, my Dad was an over-the-road trucker and was gone a lot. When he was home, he mainly slept. But he was quite pleasant and easy to be around. My Dad left my mom when I was 11 because he had "come out of the closet", revealing he was gay. They filed for divorce when I was 12. After that, I saw even less of him until I was an adult. But growing up, it was my Mother who was there for my brother and me. Our mother was a very open-minded person who believed deeply in God, angels, and spirits. She would sometimes talk to God, Jesus, or the spirit of a deceased loved one. To my recollection, she was basically simply about love. She was not one to push her beliefs on anyone, including her children. She would be happy to share what she believed but thought it was important that even her own children ultimately decide for themselves what they believed. I've always appreciated that about my mother!

Those first few years after my Dad left were pretty tough. As an adult, I now understand that my mother was in a lot of pain. Well, pain may be an understatement. She was metaphorically cut to the core, basically destroyed inside. At that time, her hurt was often taken out on me being the oldest. As a child, I didn't understand why she was always so hard on me. I did my best to step up! For a kid, I held up pretty well. I tried so hard to make life as easy as I could for my mother and brother but she would still get so upset with me. I took on more responsibility, being the default man of the house. I had to watch out for my younger brother, make sure chores got done, and cook dinner since my mother worked full time. As an adult, having been through heartbreak and life altering transitions, I now understand what my mom was going through. She was devastated, lost, and confused.

When my Dad first left home, I was in the 6th grade. I initially became deeply depressed and withdrew into myself.

This once happy, outgoing kid now became quiet and despondent. This was the time I first came to believe that much of the world was quite ugly, kids and adults alike. Despite the difficult time I had with my teacher in the 5th grade, it was when my parents split up that this rather difficult negative shift happened. I was a chubby kid who got chubbier in junior high. Though I was teased in elementary school, the worst years were between the 6th grade especially through the 7th and 8th grades in junior high school. I was often told I was ugly, fat, and stupid often in colorful ways. I wasn't athletically inclined at all. I was the last or near the last in almost every athletic test. I was such a sensitive child that getting picked on upset me terribly. Come junior high, I was picked on or bullied often. I came to dread going to school. I never wanted to fight. Frankly, it scared me. Especially as a small child, I didn't want to hurt anyone, even when they hurt me. Generally speaking, I was a nice kid. I liked people and just wanted to be liked. I still liked having fun and seeing people be happy. I didn't want any form of hardships or arguments. I just wanted "happy". I certainly wasn't perfect, but did my best not to get into trouble with my mom, the school, or with anyone.

Although I upheld my responsibilities at home, I wasn't doing well in school. My new-found disillusionment in life and the world was taking its toll on me. I became increasingly unhappy as I completely withdrew from everything and everyone. I became rather disliked by many classmates, hence the worst bullying I ever experienced. Looking back, they were just children who didn't understand why I was always so depressed. They just saw a very negative and vulnerable kid. It surely made them uncomfortable. I didn't understand how to deal with the hurt or being picked on, so I continued to withdraw deeper and deeper into myself. Sometimes, not knowing what else to do, I would cry. That just made everything worse. It seemed to be a self-perpetuating downward spiral.

I was in junior high when the divorce became final. This led to my mother's low point and perhaps the lowest point of my childhood. Home life was intense. I was always doing my best to avoid saying something to set my mom off. I became further depressed and withdrawn at home too. The bullying only got worse. I went to a junior high school that, back then, was known as a bit of "tough" school. Fights were a common occurrence among other activities. I was proportionately at my chubbiest point in regard to my height versus weight. I remember at the start of my 8th grade year, the teachers in gym class measured and weighed the students. I checked in at 5'5" and weighed 195 lbs. (To offer some perspective, I'm currently 6'4" and weigh about 185 lbs.) Bullying reached a fever pitch. 7th grade was rough but 8th grade was the worst. I was being picked on daily by many of the other kids. It was often groups of them picking on me and sometimes beating me up. Both my home life and school life were miserable. I was getting bullied at school and yelled at by my Mom at home. My brother and I were also dealing with the adjustment of the divorce. All I knew was that I was always in incredible pain inside. I had no idea what to do about it. For that matter, I couldn't have explained if I tried. I felt completely helpless. I saw no options but to somehow persevere. I grew to truly hate life! If there was a time I would escape into my dreams, it was then. Having said that, dreaming was the one thing that got me through that whole experience. I had someplace where I could be happy.

The last week of my 8th grade year I finally stood up for myself and beat up a kid who was one of my worst bullies. That year gym was my last class of the day. Class had just ended. We were in the locker room and getting dressed from our gym clothes to our street clothes. He came up behind me and grabbed and twisted my fat roll over my right hip. Naturally it hurt as it is a tender spot to get grabbed even if you're skinny.

He said one of his insulting witticisms. This time, instead of cowering in fear, I lost my temper for the first time in my life! Now mind you, I sincerely had not so much as had the thought of hurting him let alone starting a fight with him. I wasn't one of those bullied kids dreaming about some kind of revenge. I really just wanted to get along with everyone. No matter, at the moment, I "went for it"! I spun around, hit him, and knocked him to the floor! I kept hitting him until the teacher came and pulled me off. At that moment, I grasped what I had just done. I couldn't believe it! It all felt surreal. That's when the fear set in that a potentially severe punishment was inevitable from the school and my mom. I had a fear of being suspended. There were only a few days left in the school year, so that would have meant tacking on an extra day or two or more. I sure didn't want to have to explain that to my mom. I couldn't imagine the trouble I would have been in with her. I also had a fear of a reprisal. I thought for sure that the bully and some of his friends were going to get back at me. I figured school life would be worse than ever.

The teacher took me into his office after the fight. He said that he knew that the kids "had been hard on me all year" so he was going to defer any suspension. He said if it happened again, I would get double. Believe me, I seriously appreciated that! While I have had favorite teachers over the years that I will always remember. I will definitely always remember him for that.

The next day, everything seemed different. I shook off the fear of the kids. I realized I truly had "had it" and didn't care what happened. I had decided that win or lose, outnumbered or not, I was going to fight no matter what if they messed with me! Strangely, my bully was now afraid of me. There was no reprisal as anticipated. I was genuinely surprised by this. I learned I could stand up for myself and that sometimes it was ok to do so. The bullying stopped even with all the other kids that had also been bullying me in other school settings. This was a moment where I shifted, learning a lesson about myself and people, especially those who are in a school environment. During this time of my life, I was fully convinced that there was no God. I hated myself and I hated being alive. Sadly, yes, at this young age, I started to contemplate suicide. There were many nights I went to sleep wishing I wouldn't wake up. The only thing that stopped me was me a terrible fear of death. This, in spite of the "ghostly" experiences I had, was something I couldn't quite comprehend. These experiences were far removed from my thoughts at this point as I had rationalized them away. I could only identify with the five senses. Even my dreams at this point had turned more about money, big houses, and lots of cars. I was just going to have what was mine, as far as I was concerned.

Given my atheistic beliefs I thought death would just be an end of everything as in non-existence. I found that prospect disconcerting. I tended to go between the thought of which was worse, my life or death? Given how much I thought about dying, it was the fear of the unknown that won out.

Fortunately, it also helped that there were a handful of my mother's friends who had reached out to me in friendship, which I did appreciate. There were some wonderful people in our life back then! It was nice to have people, even though I was a kid and they were adults, to hang out with and actually be friends. It did make a difference! I appreciate each of those people! It sounds kind of funny to say for a kid who is just coming out of junior high school that most of his friends were adults.

These awesome friends helped me to make my life feel worthwhile at times. However, though this seems like a dichotomy, there were people, often adults, who would confide in me. One thing I was good at, even then, was empathizing and tuning into what a person needs for insight and help. Even though I didn't know how to help myself, I liked to help others and had a knack for it. Though I still didn't believe in God and feared death, I read about astrology and other forms of occult. It's hard to say why, other than to say that some part of me, despite my pain, knew there was something "more" to life and our existence. These friend connections helped me to see that others had ideas and beliefs about spirituality and the divine. It encouraged me to at least keep an open mind.

When I got to high school, things started to turn around for the better. My mother also came out of her own hardships. She was finally able to leave the past behind and start to enjoy the life we had. Money was tight but life was generally good! While like any family, we had our "moments", she really became a light in many lives including me, my brother, and many of our friends. She was my best friend and my brother's too, while still being mom. She seemed to balance that off well. I went to a fairly big high school with a lot of amenities. Yes, it had some "city" elements to it. There seemed to be a fight just about every day somewhere in the school. I don't recall any guns but some people got stabbed, clubbed, and other such things. Plus, you could get just about any drug. There were also positives about the school. While I liked sports, I also enjoyed theater and choir. This school had one of the best choirs and theater departments in Michigan. I really got into that. I felt I was starting to find my way. I liked school once I got to high school. I had lots of friends and things to do that I enjoyed.

I will point out that, despite all the things that certainly weren't exactly positives for me growing up in Michigan, I did have some great friends as a child with many great memories. This is especially true with some of the kids in my neighborhood where I spent most of my years while living in Michigan! I was grateful for this part of my life! We had a lot of fun playing backyard football, baseball, basketball, and street hockey. We also had some awesome games of "Flashlight Tag". I had a great time in northern Michigan motorcycling in the summer and snowmobiling in the winter. Michigan has hundreds, maybe thousands of miles of trails. Those were some of my best times! My mom took me to some awesome shows with her friends. Even as a kid, I got to go some big concerts. I rarely saw other kids my age there so I thought it was pretty special that I got to go. I think I was 13 when I want to my first big concert in addition to seeing my first live club show. The first was Stephen Stills from Crosby, Stills, Nash, and sometimes Young. It was at a venue called Pine Knob which holds about 15,000 people. It was half under a pavilion and half on a grass hill beyond the pavilion area. People could bring blankets and sit under the stars enjoying a show. We were on the hill for Stephen Stills. I just thought that was the coolest thing! Plus, I never imagined such a big sound as a live concert sized sound system in some place that big. I was enthralled. I saw Bob Seger, who was...and still is...an all-time favorite of mine. What a phenomenal show! The crowd was totally energized dancing and screaming throughout the whole show. Bob genuinely puts his heart and soul into his performances. He was always known for doing that. I saw him again in Denver in the mid 80's. Every person in the place was on their feet the whole show and singing every word to every song. Bob Seger and the Silver Bullet Band were among my favorite artists to see live! I saw the Doobie Brothers, Kansas, Sha Na, Dr. Hook, and a handful of others. These shows were so much fun! I would scream, clap, and dance along with just about everybody else. The Doobie's were just amazing musicians and had such a cool way about them. Sha Na and their whole 50's motif was a blast! They really got the crowd hopping. Among the most entertaining of the shows was the Beach Boys. They had so much energy it was unreal! Lead singer, Mike Love, was all over the stage and even in the crowd. That was such a memorable show. I also saw a handful of other great shows while still in Michigan. It was one of my favorite things about my time living there especially since there weren't generally other kids my age at these shows. I want to point out that Detroit was and is a great music city!

While I did play some football, and was in some bowling leagues, I liked playing baseball the best. As I've said, I wasn't very athletic as a kid, but I was a solid baseball player. My favorite position was catcher. I was pretty good at it. Hence, why I sometimes daydreamed about being a pro baseball player. As a chubby kid during the time I was in Michigan, I made a good target to keep the ball from getting past me in the event of an errant pitch. I also had a good arm for throwing out a runner trying to steal second base. It's a good distance from home plate to second base. As a catcher, it's an important throw to be able to make accurately. Plus, the ball has to get thrown quickly. I could quickly jump up and make the throw without having to take a step. As a catcher, you just jump up and throw. And I was a good long ball hitter. It was a good thing too since I wasn't a very fast runner. Frankly I was rather slow. As in gym class, I was usually one of, if not, the slowest runner on any team I was on. Some of the ball parks we played in didn't have a "home run" fence. For the ones that did, I hit a fair number over the fence for a home run. That was nice because I could jog around the bases without speed being a factor. In the event there was no fence, I would have to hit the ball a long way out to have a chance of getting around the bases. Hits that would be a home run for any other kid were generally a triple at best for me. Anyway, I had a lot of fun playing baseball!

My mother's brother, Bill, was integral in my life especially while living in Michigan. One of my all-time favorite memories growing up in Michigan was with him. As a kid, I had dreamed of being a radio DJ. My uncle was fairly well connected. He had a friend, unfortunately I don't recall his name, who was a station manager for a now defunct radio station called W4. At that point, it was a rock station. Howard

Stern was the morning DJ. This, Howard's time working at W4, was actually featured in his movie, "Howard Stern, Private Parts". This was before he blew up to the icon he has become in the entertainment industry today. I used to listen to him every morning as I was getting ready for school. I thought he was a total laugh riot and there was always some good Rock & Roll with him doing something funny. Uncle Bill knew I was a fan. For my 13th birthday present, he made arrangements to take me out of school on a weekday morning and go to the W4 radio station. He set up a personal tour of the station with his station manager friend. It was during Howard's morning show. It was one of the most awesome things ever! I was beyond excited! Uncle Bill's friend was very friendly and took his time with me in showing me around and answered all my questions. I learned a ton from that tour. It inspired my dream to be a DJ.

Yes, I did get to meet Howard. It was part of the tour. I got to spend a little time with him when a set of music was playing and he wasn't live. He was very open and friendly. I remember being excited that he was so nice to me! He and I talked for a few minutes. He was very encouraging and said, "Maybe one day we'll do a radio show together" as I shook his hand before walking out of the studio. It hasn't happened but I would welcome the opportunity. ...just "sayin'"!

My Uncle Bill was friends with Punch Andrews who was the manager for Bob Seger. Bob's "Night Moves" album had just been released. That was the follow up to the "Live Bullet" album that helped Bob turn the corner into becoming a national artist. I had wanted that album so much. Well, Uncle Bill had gotten me that album and the, at the time, brand new "Night Moves" album. Plus, he had gotten Punch to get a poster signed by Bob Seger saying, "Rex, all the best and happy birthday!". I kept that poster for years. Unfortunately, after several moves and many years of hanging on my bedroom walls, it eventually fell apart. I am a fan of Corvettes because of my Uncle Bill, largely because he owned several. It was always such a total blast to go out driving with him. He wasn't afraid to punch the gas from time to time. He gave me some nice tastes of what those cars could do. It was always so awesome! To this day, I still love Vettes! Uncle Bill was a great guy and a big positive for me and my life growing up! He passed away in 1997. What a beautiful human being he was!!

Growing up, like for most kids, was often very painful and difficult. But while the time in Michigan certainly had its hard times, there were certainly some good times with some great people too! However, early in my sophomore year, my mother, brother and I moved to Colorado.

**

Through it all, I still wasn't sure what to think about my belief of God and spirituality. Even though I had those "hard to explain" experiences I basically just put them out of my mind. I hadn't thought about them for a long time. I chalked them up to them being some distant dream or "who knows what... and who cares!" But my curiosity grew as I continued to feel that there had to be something more...

When we moved to Colorado, we moved to a small town a little ways north of Colorado Springs and about 45 minutes' drive south of Denver called Palmer Lake. While it was and is a beautiful little town and we had a nice little house on the side of the mountain with a nice view, the school was lacking in some key amenities I had in the school in Michigan. Plus, going from suburban Detroit and a good size school to a rather small town and school was quite the change. This was all so different from Detroit. Moving to Palmer Lake was initially a bit of a culture shock to me. My school in Colorado was good academically but it was quite small then, with maybe 400 students from the 9th to 12th grade. The area and school have grown and are much bigger nowadays. My class at my school in Michigan was bigger than the entire school I went to in Colorado. I believe there were at least 500 in my class alone at my high school in Michigan.

The first week after I started at the new school, I let loose some of my "Detroit attitude" with one of the "popular" kids. I was used to the big city way of doing things and perhaps still had a bit of a preemptive reaction from the years I was bullied. In hindsight, what the kid said was no big deal and I clearly overreacted. The kid said something insulting to me and I threatened to "kick his ass". I suggested we meet some place after school and fight. He and the other kids all laughed at me. I really didn't know how to react to that. I had become accustomed to the occasional "butting of heads" with some guy not being a big deal. In Detroit, you talk your stuff, usually it doesn't go anywhere, and you forget about it. No big deal. To my new classmates, however, the attitude thing made quite an impression. Unfortunately for me, it wasn't a good one. There was no fight but he and the other kids who witnessed it clearly thought I was a jerk. Fights at that school were pretty far and few between. Needless to say, I was so excited to have my one chance to be the "new kid" and it had to start like that. I didn't have an easy time making friends at that school at first. I was pretty disappointed with the whole thing at that point.

The school in Colorado didn't offer certain things I liked or for which I excelled. While I enjoyed sports like baseball and football, I tended to prefer theater and choir, although I may have been reluctant to admit that at the time. The school in Colorado barely had a theater department and a very small choir. There was always a shortage of boys. I remember once when we were putting on a musical we had to go and recruit a couple of boys to fill out the cast. It wasn't a question of who did the best at the audition but rather who was simply willing to play a role. While fun, and I did enjoy everyone in the cast, it wasn't quite the same level as my Michigan school and wasn't taken as seriously. My school in Michigan had its own theater, a full drama department, and a full music department. The choirs in the Michigan school consisted of beginning boys' and beginning girls' choirs, a concert choir mixed with boys and girls, and a couple of specialty groups. They also had huge turnouts for any type of show or choral group. Again, it was an adjustment. Thankfully, the kids I performed with in the Colorado school were awesome! I did make some good friends.

I "tackled" (couldn't resist) playing football both in Michigan and in Colorado. That didn't go so well. I had my biggest growth spurt going into my freshman year while still in Michigan. My ankles weren't too strong. I ended up badly spraining both of them and missed most of that season. The football team there was pretty competitive, typically making the playoffs. I got to Colorado midway through the football season in my new school. I joined the team which didn't go so well either. It took a little time to get used to the altitude and it was a pretty uneventful season. The team lost almost every game in JV and Varsity. I never felt that I fit in there though I made some friends. I also didn't much like the head coach and he didn't like me. I wanted very much to play baseball. But the same coach who coached football was the same coach who coached baseball. Needless to say, I never played baseball at that school. The move, while best for my family at the time, was initially disappointing to me. The perception that I didn't have much to look forward to at this school, or by being in Colorado, sent me right back into my depression. I was wishing that we could have stayed in Michigan.

When I had gotten to my Colorado school, I was so completely within myself and my limited perspective of reality that I couldn't recognize something potentially life-changing right in front of me. What little experience I had with girls my age at that point was pretty much negative stemming from junior high. I was laughed at when saying "hi" to a girl I had a crush on, among other similarly humiliating experiences. In my sophomore year, I was in my new school feeling completely out of place. I hadn't asked a girl to a dance since junior high. I had a part-time job working as a dishwasher/prep cook. I liked the staff. Most of the time, we had fun working together. One of my favorite co-workers was a girl named Lisa. She was a senior on the Pom-Pom squad at school and a generally fun positive person. We got along great! One day at work Lisa tells me that her friend Julie likes me, and that I should ask her out. ...did I mention Julie was a senior and head cheerleader? Wow, talk about the stuff of my dreams! I couldn't believe it, Julie likes me?! Now understand, Julie wasn't the stereotypical "popular girl, cheerleader". Not only was she beautiful and smart, but she was a genuinely sweet person. She was nice to everyone! She was popular for good reason. Needless to say, it didn't take long before I was rationalizing to myself that Lisa had to be wrong, Julie's not interested in me. In hindsight, I see Julie was being shy around me. That's not uncommon when a person has a crush on another. I simply should have stepped up and asked her out. But my perception was she wasn't acting interested so she couldn't really be interested. I never asked her out.

My anger began to grow during these years, though I kept it to mostly to myself. That was sometimes difficult. On a few occasions, I would break something or punch or kick an inanimate object out of anger. I spent a lot of time escaping into listening to music and into my daydreams. I generally felt bored and apathetic. Not from the lack of things to do or the friends I did have. Everything just felt empty. I never dated in high school, though not from the lack of trying. During my sophomore year, I joined wrestling. I was at my highest weight of about 250 lbs. No, it wasn't muscle. I had gotten taller but was still rather chubby. By the end of wrestling season, I had lost over 80 lbs and was under 170 lbs. I've been skinny ever since. Regardless, I was pretty much down on life and myself. I didn't like school. The adjustment to the small town, while a beautiful town, was hard for me. I just yearned for something more urban, and more to the point, Detroit. I just resided in this cesspool of dark empty feelings again pulling back into myself escaping into dreams.

I had come to believe a demon had attached itself to me. I wasn't sure how or why. But something that felt heavy and dark seemed to be somehow manifesting itself in me. Interesting thought for an atheist, or perhaps agnostic. Somehow, I could feel a distinct presence. Yes, it "freaked me out"! I could feel it manipulating me, opening some internal doors and drawing out this nasty dark sludge that was deep inside me. While it felt like a separate consciousness, I felt a connection. In a way, it felt like me but somehow wasn't. It was like being connected and displaced at the same time. I began feeling increasing levels of anger with an anxiety I had not experienced before. I wasn't entirely sure why. I couldn't put my finger on anything substantive beyond my feelings. Though I was disappointed with the way things had gone thus far in Colorado, there didn't seem to be any reason to be harboring this level of growing anger. It was like something was influencing me and the situations around me. However, this wasn't anger toward anyone in particular but rather mostly to myself. Something about calling it a demon seemed to fit. I didn't have and couldn't think of any other word for it. I had felt that this demon would sabotage certain key parts of my life from within, sabotaging my perceptions and thereby my decisions. This was especially true when it came to something I wanted, like a girl on whom I had a crush. I seemed to have this pattern of going for the girl who I couldn't have. Perhaps a "knee-jerk" reaction to missing an opportunity with Julie. In hindsight, I realize there were some great girls that liked me and may well have dated me. But I completely missed them in my increasingly pessimistic, closed-in mind. I couldn't perceive these possibilities as being part of my reality. I seemed to be in state of "tunnel vision". I felt I was a victim of "Murphy's law". I always felt like if something could go wrong, it would. I would reference that often. If I wanted it, it wasn't going to happen. I was compelled, unknowingly at the time, to be ensconced in my limited perception of my reality and any opportunities that may have existed. I would continually make the wrong decisions in setting myself up for disappointment over and over again. I truly felt somehow cursed in my oblivion to my pattern. The thing about being in a dark space is that I was basically wearing some pretty serious blinders. There was so much I just didn't see. The blinders clouded and obscured the big picture, especially in making the best decision for the best course of action in my life at the time. This became a vicious downward cycle in putting out and attracting dark energies. Life felt like it became very dark very fast. Mind you, this is different from when I was in junior high going through the hardships of the divorce and being picked on. That was painful and difficult but somehow didn't carry the dark feelings of this later time. As such, I would occasionally comment about "my demon".

Once we were having a get-together with friends at our house. I had chosen to go to bed early. My bedroom was downstairs. A girl friend of mine needed to use the bathroom. We had a bathroom upstairs and down. The upstairs bathroom was being used so she decided to come downstairs. No one was down there except me as I had just laid down to sleep. The whole downstairs was dark. I remember hearing someone start to come down the stairs then turn around and go back up. It turns out it was my friend. The next day she took me aside to tell me she was scared for me. She explained to me why she didn't use the downstairs bathroom the night before. She told me she felt an overwhelming fear as she started down the stairs. She said she felt the presence of a demon. She said it felt so strong that she couldn't come down. She preferred to wait until the other bathroom opened up. She was genuinely afraid! I had explained to her that I knew about it and that it was "my demon". She advised me to find help. She expressed she was very concerned for me.

I still had no real concrete belief in God but was a bit fascinated with the occult. There was at least a modicum of spirituality percolating within me. During junior high, I was basically an atheist. I was convinced there was no such thing as God. By high school, I had become more agnostic, having at least an openness to the possibilities however remote. Every once in a while, I found myself talking to God and those that had passed like my mother did. Even though I was still young, I had already experienced death of loved ones and close friends quite a few times. Looking back, partly because of the passing of people I loved, I was starting to open myself to the possibilities of what may lie beyond this life. It didn't feel right they should simply perish. I would feel perplexed sometimes thinking, "this flesh and blood can't be all there is," but I didn't have an idea of how to elaborate on that.

It was during this time that I first realized just how empathic I was. I realized I was feeling other people's feelings like they were my own. I couldn't explain how or why and quite simply didn't understand it. Yet, throughout my life, I often felt overwhelmed with crazy unpredictable mood swings. Sometimes I just felt like I was all over the place emotionally. I went so far as to think that there was yet something else that was wrong with me. Yes, some of it stemmed from the hurt and depression I had felt, and maybe from this so-called demon. I came to realize I was also taking on a multitude of feelings from those around me.

One early morning in high school came a major realization of just how empathetic I was. During the beginning of my senior year, I was watching cheerleader tryouts. Like many young boys, I liked watching pretty girls. They took place in the school commons area/cafeteria in the mornings before classes started. Anyone could watch. I remember watching and becoming increasingly anxious and agitated with each girl's tryout. Some were easier to watch than others depending on how good and confident they were. But regardless I was feeling all these girls' feelings no matter what. There was a pivotal moment when it all dawned on me. The "crowning blow" was watching a very cute girl step up for her turn. I didn't know her but had seen her around school. She was clearly terribly nervous. Her voice was shaky when she spoke. I could feel how much she wanted to do well and be chosen to be a cheerleader. I couldn't help but root for her. As she began, she immediately made a mistake followed by another and another. You didn't have to be an empath for this to be painful to watch. She was becoming increasingly distraught as she did her routine to the point of being on the verge of tears as she finished. She was trying hard to hold back the tears and smile, but she was clearly crushed. She knew, as everyone watching did, that there was no way she going to be picked to be a cheerleader. She knew it had gone poorly. I too felt profoundly crushed as I watched her do her routine most intently, like I was trying to somehow help her in my mind, hoping so much she would pull it together. She didn't. She eventually apologized to the cheerleading coaches and captains who were to decide on the JV and Varsity squads. She then ran off. I found myself struggling to hold back tears as if I had experienced this with her. I had to run to the bathroom because I had teared up. I had to take a few minutes to collect myself. After that I couldn't watch the tryouts anymore. That was the first time I realized that I was not only feeling another's feelings, I could also feel the emotional tone set by the event itself with all the girls going through some form of anticipation, anxiety, and/or nervousness. I couldn't believe I was really taking on all these feelings during the cheerleader tryouts. The whole experience was incredibly dynamic, quite the enlightening revelation! These feelings were sparking something inside me that added to my perception or picture of my reality. In a way, I imagine it's like a person being blind all their life suddenly being able to see. It all now made sense. Such a realization will change one's reality as it did mine. Moving forward everything felt different. I liked it once I started to understand it!

Realizing I could be so acutely empathetic to others answered a lot of questions with respect to all the confusing feelings throughout my life to that point. I started paying close attention to the feelings I was getting throughout the course of a day. I began to differentiate between my own feelings and feelings that belonged to someone else. I even began to learn how to "filter" out certain feelings and energies. It helped to be more internally organized and not always be feeling so confused and overwhelmed.

I was already "that person" people came to talk to when they wanted help in working something out. I was then and am now "the keeper of secrets". Anyone who has ever opened up to me has known it would always stay between us. I was always able to tune into a person and whatever situation they were describing and often times offer some helpful insight. I still wasn't sure what to do with this new-found attribute, other than help friends. But it inspired my dreams and maybe had some ability to be helpful to others. While being empathetic has sometimes been difficult, this self-knowledge was life-changing in the most positive ways especially given what was still to come.

As a senior in high school, I spent about a year's time talking with a psychology professional named Gale. He wasn't technically a spiritualist per se, but I think he must have been a spiritual person. He was certainly open-minded. He was technically just a licensed clinical social worker. While he didn't carry the educational accolades of others in the psychology field, he was immensely helpful for me. I believe he was quite intuitive and deep. Gale had a gift! In my endeavor to seek a balance with my sense of empathy and the insights it allotted me, it helped immensely to be able to talk to someone about it. I could share anything I wanted to without judgement. We also talked about other things like my demon, death, and the divorce. Even though it had been several years and my family and I had put it behind us, it was nice to "air out" all of that. He helped me to find a certain peace and balance with all those feelings. Gale had a genuine ability to "tune-in" and to offer guidance without talking at me or "preaching" to me. He had a knack for explaining things pragmatically and for asking the right questions so I could find my own answers. He helped me to understand many things about my feelings and mood swings. Because I could talk to him about pretty much anything, he also helped me to organize my thoughts and feelings in a way where I could apply some of his suggestions and handle these empathic feelings. To this day, I still appreciate him! This time spent with him proved helpful throughout many points of my life!

My new-found realization of being empathetic had another important aspect to it. I realized this is why I felt everything with such a distinction and clarity. This isn't to suggest that I feel any more or less than anyone else, only that it was always so pronounced. For the first time, I was able to create a perspective for the interpretation of these feelings in applying it to my everyday life. This was a positive step in evolving my dreams. I was spending time in deep quiet contemplation, daydreaming these thoughts and feelings. This was a key step in my spiritual growth.

I was starting to have insights and ways of thinking about things I never had before, especially about death. By this point in my life, I had experienced death of some I was close to and some I knew more casually. By the age of 13, all my grandparents had passed away (my grandpa on my mother's side died before I was born). As a freshman in high school, I heard what happened to a kid I knew in junior high who was a track athlete. I did not know him too well but we had a couple of classes before going to separate high schools. I remember him being a nice guy. I heard he had run a 100-meter dash during a track practice and just as he finished, he had a heart attack. He collapsed and died on the spot. With him, it wasn't so much about grieving. Like I said, we weren't that close. Given my experience with Jeff dying as a little kid, this death struck me because while older, he too was a kid. Something about being the same age and considering that he was an athlete was just hard to accept. As an athlete, I wouldn't have thought of him as someone whose heart would just stop. It bothered me, because I now understood that anyone could die at any time, including me. When Jeff died, perhaps from the perspective of a little kid, that possibility didn't even occur to me.

I started to look at death in a different way. I was becoming less fearful of my own death. I realized that death unto itself wasn't necessarily a bad thing. To lose a loved one to death was something that was still potentially "difficult" to experience for those of us still here on Earth. Losing someone you love or that special family pet can be most devastating and take months or years to get over. Some people never really "get over" such a death. But I was starting to believe that death unto itself wasn't bad for the person dying. Yes, the process of dying may sometimes be long and painful, but the part of leaving this body and moving beyond our life here somehow resonated as being peaceful. My mom had a friend who passed because of cancer. I didn't personally know him very well but it was the first time I saw someone go through the process of deteriorating towards his death because of the cancer. It wasn't easy to witness but clearly it was far tougher for him to go through it. This was something I felt I needed to pay attention to. It was intense! I have immense respect for him. I can't say what happened "behind closed doors", but I never heard him complain. Each time I saw him, he was always positive. Though I wasn't personally too close to him, being a part of this experience did impact me. I learned some big lessons with his passing and got, for me, a totally different perspective on death. Up to this point, I had thought experiencing the death of a loved one was supposed to be a sad, somber experience. Funerals were supposed to be very serious. I went to his funeral and wake. The funeral had lots of tears as he was clearly loved, but the wake was a "straight up" party! It was rather mind-expanding for me. I heard lots of wonderful stories about the deceased. There were lots of laughs and lots of drinks. I thought it was pretty cool but I was a bit surprised. I would never have thought about throwing a party for a wake. Novel idea!

I was talking to my mother about this the next day. She explained that this was an Irish wake. She told me that the tears were for the funeral service, but the wake was meant to be a celebration of the person's life and passing. She said "everyone should be sent to Heaven in style". She also explained that when she dies she wants to "go out" the same way. It was important that family and friends celebrate the love and good times and have fun when she passes! That made total sense to me. This experience provided me an important insight and perspective on death and dying.

Through all the ups and downs, I didn't care about school. The sooner I was out the better! If it wasn't for my mother, I would have dropped out for sure. She was on me hard to graduate high school. Saying "No, I'm dropping out" to mom wasn't an option. Fortunately, I did graduate high school. I did have some genuine friends. For as hard as those years were for me there also lots of happy memories! There was a group of people with whom I had a lot of fun! As my brother got older, as did his friends, I found some true friendships there too. Ultimately, my mom's friends, my brother's friends, and my friends all got along and sometimes all hung out together. On my birthday in my senior year, I was given a Halloween birthday party at my house (that's right, my birthday is on Halloween). My mom and all my friends planned it. I had another, completely "out of left field" experience with a girl named Kim. She was a dance student at Colorado College and a hostess at the restaurant I was working at during that time. She was a rather elegant and beautiful 19 year old woman! Being single, she was always getting hit on. I remember the hotel manager was a young good-looking guy who drove a Porsche. He tried to get her to go out with him. She had no interest in him or anyone. As for me, I finally had found the nerve to ask a couple of girls to dances and prom my junior year. Each one said no. So, I wasn't feeling terribly confident in myself. Not that I ever really was. I got stuck working my birthday. Kim was working that night. The work just seemed to be piling up. I was becoming concerned I would miss my own birthday party. Kim and I always had a great rapport. I was taking a five-minute break and she joined me. I told her about my party and wanting to get there. I knew she would be getting off soon. I casually mentioned that she was welcome to come if she wanted to. I thought nothing of it. It was more me just being polite. I didn't think she would go. I went back to work and my friend co-worker, Kerry, knew of my situation and told me to go. He would finish my shift for me. I was so grateful! I thanked him maybe 10 times! I went to the bathroom to clean up quickly the best I could and changed my clothes. As I was getting ready to leave, Kim found me. She said that she was about to get off and that she was looking forward to going to the party with me... as in, my date! I think I stuttered and stammered for a few seconds, seemed like an eternity. I eventually gathered myself up enough to say something like, "Great!" She really liked me! I definitely did NOT see that coming!

Sigh... while Kim and I went out a few times I basically managed to sabotage and end the relationship that was growing. We totally connected. When I wasn't being horribly insecure and immature, I thought she among the most incredible girls I had ever known! Again, I couldn't let myself believe that she could like me, let alone maybe love me. After a couple months, it was the holidays. I was pretty disappointed with myself over how I treated her especially since I was still really bummed that I didn't ask Julie out a couple years earlier. I couldn't believe I had done it again, only this time I knew I really hurt someone because we did spend some time together. I decided to reach out to her to apologize for how I treated her. I had no misconceptions that she would go out with me again, but I had to at least apologize. It was important that I convey how beautiful and wonderful I really believed she was! I would have been happy if we could have just been friends. It turns out that she was on vacation at that time and was killed in a car accident! I could imagine how crushed her family must have been, but that really twisted me up inside! I couldn't believe it! I would never get to tell her what I had hoped to.

I first started DJing during those high school years in Colorado. I always liked playing music when friends were over at the house. People always seemed to enjoy my selections. As I think about it, it was my senior year when the opportunity presented itself to DJ for a school dance. I DJ'd two, maybe three dances. Lots of people always danced and had fun! It was such a rush! I was hooked from that point on. I still like to DJ even now. One of the best feelings in the world for me is being an integral piece to people dancing and having fun! But at the time, I was just too depressed, angry, and down on myself to sincerely appreciate the positives way I could have. The good feelings never lasted for long. I recognize now that there were many missed opportunities during these years.

I will say that I had one of the all-time epic graduation parties of the 20th century! Ok, maybe just the decade, but it was the best time I'd ever had as a young man! Never mind being beyond elated to have graduated high school, I was so ready to have a party! The party totally rocked! It was held at my mother's then boyfriend's house. We had a full house with everybody dancing. People were indoors, outdoors, upstairs, and downstairs. Everybody was dancing and cheering! My mother's boyfriend was a musician. Some of his musician friends came over and jammed. They played some great stuff in getting people moving! I played music during the band's breaks to keep people dancing. At one point, I was dancing my heart out, outside in the front yard with a number of friends. Again, what a great party! That is definitely a memory I will always cherish!

After I graduated, I seemed to lighten up a bit about myself. I seemed to be getting into a positive vibe with my life. After a couple of temporary or seasonal jobs, I had a good job in Colorado Springs in a factory making computer drives and was making decent money while still living at home in Palmer Lake. Over the summer, one of my best long-time brothers named Gary and I "ran the tables" at beach volleyball on Monument Lake beach. He was a sort of adopted son of my mom and a brother to me. After all these years, he still is. To keep this in perspective, it certainly wasn't volleyball like you'll find on an LA beach. Given I'm from Michigan, as nice as it was to have a body of water like Monument Lake to swim, it was tiny compared to just about any inland Michigan lake and some of the ponds. Also, as far as beaches go, there wasn't exactly the nice soft beach sand you might find on a "real" beach. It was a little tough on the feet. It took some getting used to. But no matter, it was a busy place. There were lots of people who lived in the area going for a day in the water when it got hot. It was nice to get in the water and have some fun swimming especially for a Michigander who was missing the water. The Colorado Rockies are quite beautiful! No matter how homesick I would get, I always loved the Rocky Mountains! That definitely helped! At the beach, there were several pavilions where private parties were held. There was a lot going on at this little lake especially on the weekends. There were, I think, three volleyball nets set up, close to competition height. So at least it resembled a real volleyball experience. Volleyball seemed to be a popular past time. Lots of people played. One time, early in the summer season, Gary, some friends, and I were playing two-on-two volleyball. Gary and I teamed up. We played our friends and eventually we were playing other people on the beach two-on-two. Gary and I kept winning. Eventually we were taking all challengers. We basically "ran the table" all summer. I can't recall for sure if we lost any games. But if we did, it was few and far between. That was a fun summer!

Death was becoming less something to fear and more something to be embraced. I was now again becoming fascinated with death. I felt I wanted to understand it. But although I had learned different ways to look at the experience of death, I certainly didn't understand it. Nonetheless, I made a decision that I hope when I die that everyone can celebrate my life and death. By the time I was approaching 18 years of age, I found I was making peace with my own mortality. This level of thinking was strongly perpetuated by my newfound understanding of my inclination for empathy. I was also fortunate to have a great licensed clinical social worker, aka Gale, to talk to.

One of the coolest things my mother did for me was get me an astrological natal chart reading as an 18th birthday present. It was from someone who was a good friend of my mother's, a talented reader named Coreen. She had read for my mom many times over the years. My mother had an immense respect for her! Though I didn't know Coreen well, having only met her a handful of times, I rather liked her. I was super excited to get this reading. Simply put, a natal chart reading is based on the movements of the planets and stars in relation to us along the path of our lives starting with the moment of birth. It is quite complex and can be used to break down a potential path of a person's entire life. The natal chart is comprised of our birth sign or sun sign, a rising sign, moon sign, and 12 houses of influence. These are possibilities based on decisions we make throughout the course of a life especially at certain key, life-altering points. I'm not nearly qualified to explain beyond that but this reading covered the pathway of my whole life.

Coreen was incredibly insightful. She explained so many things about my life up to that point. She was quite accurate and her insights made sense. I knew there was seriously something to this practice especially in the hands of someone as skilled as Coreen. Given all the years that have passed, I now have a vantage point in my life where I can further gauge the entirety of the reading. I can look back, as I recall things that she said, and see how much of it has aligned with what has happened. Even now I can recall things she said that resonate to where I am now. She even explained to me how important it is to learn to listen to "spirit" or my divine guidance. Though she didn't specifically mention my NDE, she did say (this is a paraphrase) that I'm at a point in the soul journey where karma will react much faster for the better or worse. She said that I am to do something important for the world. If I'm not moving toward this path, something that will alter the course of my entire life would happen. I realize this small snippet of what she said is relatively generic and even cliché, but she did elaborate extensively on each point. It was a 2-hour session. That would practically be a book unto itself. Suffice it to say, there have since been many parallels from my life to the readings. I still reflect on it from time to time for insight.

This was exciting to me at 18 years of age looking forward to my future and dreaming about the possibilities! While my dreams still had a big material component to them, I was once again also dreaming about how to positively impact the world. However, Coreen did suggest in the reading that much of what I dreamed about, like meeting the "love of my life" and finding my true path would materialize and come into fruition. I would have that "grow old together" experience and basically "find my way" but it would be many years later in my life. I could tell there were some things she had a hard time saying to me. But she said that there would be quite an intense growth process before being ready to fulfill my destiny, if you will. Much of the reading was hard to understand at that time because much of what she said regarding my true successes were a long way off. As a young man, I didn't see any reason to have to wait for anything. I wanted everything right away. But no matter, she gave me a lot to think about. There are things from the reading that are now clear given hindsight. For that matter, there are bits of info from the reading that are still becoming clear. This was further affirmation to trust in my insights. For the first time, I began to trust my empathy and intuition. I thought, who knows, maybe one day I can learn to do what Coreen does. What a truly gifted person, she was! It would be amazing to speak with Coreen now being on the "other side" of this experience!

One thing I want to note is that my mother was quite intuitive. She probably could have learned to give readings and do them well, if she had wanted. Needless to say, if my mother uttered the words, "I have a feeling…", whatever ensued was always right. It was rather uncanny. Naturally, it would usually be something you didn't want to hear. She did have a gift that I had to recognize. It was very real as she was consistently right.

Even our friends knew what it meant if my mother uttered those words.

I experienced my first romantic relationship when I was 19. Lori was my "first love". I think we were together shy of a year. She was a wonderful woman who was 11 years older than me. She also had two daughters, Connie and Christy. Connie, the oldest, was closer to me in age than Lori was. We all got along quite well! I became good friends with her daughters, especially Connie. I even got along great with Lori's parents. Despite the age difference with my girlfriend and me, they treated me very well. I liked them a lot. In many ways, my relationship with Lori was the kind of relationship many may wish they could have. We were close friends, laughed a lot, and talked about almost everything. Oh, and the passion was quite amazing!

Lori was religious and a strong believer in Jesus. She wasn't pushing her beliefs on people. She was quite simply a really good person. She had an endearing quality to her nature. Naturally we talked a lot about Jesus and Christianity. We had some conversations I found interesting. I went to church with her many times. I don't recall the denomination but learned some things about Jesus I didn't know before. But still I didn't "get it" during the time regarding the idea of faith. However, I did my best to keep an open mind. I had felt that no matter who Jesus really was, there was something different about him compared to other people and historical figures with whom I was familiar. I thought anyone who lived and died for what he believed in, the cause of love, was special to me!

Beyond my time in church with my first girlfriend, I was keeping a generally open mind about the possibilities spiritually. At least regarding what I had been exposed to, I was increasingly fascinated with astrology as I was seeking a means to understanding myself and others. I felt there was so much I didn't understand. However, I was also open to theories and ideas about psychic phenomena, ghosts (I had begun thinking about my past experiences again) and becoming more comfortable with the idea of death.

Beyond Christianity, astrology, and some of the bits and pieces I picked along this path, I had little knowledge of anything else of a religious or spiritual nature. I did have a certain respect and even love for this person who was Jesus. I wasn't sure about the "son of God" idea. I had thought that if there was a God then we would all be the sons and daughters of God. I also had a hard time with the idea of him "dying for our sins". My thought was if he did "wipe the karmic slate clean" for humanity, there should have some form of worldwide shift towards higher understanding that followed the crucifixion. History shows us that clearly isn't the case. My logic was that the sins of the past prior to Jesus' death should not have continued to be repeated if there was some form of higher understanding. It seemed to me, after Jesus' death, that people continued to be stuck in their ignorance repeating those same sins as history has continually been repeated. So my question became, "How can you be forgiven of sins if you're just going to continually repeat them?" That aspect of the Biblical story of Jesus had me feeling that it just didn't make sense. Regardless of my overall questions, it didn't change my feeling that Jesus was still an important historical figure. Something about him still resonated with me. I liked the idea of living life in love. Especially if he did die for his beliefs in working to make a positive change in the world, that had to be immensely respected! I wondered within myself what I would do in the same situation. Would I have that kind of integrity and strength to live and die for what I believe in? In a way, I felt I could somehow identify with Jesus as somewhat of a mentor, perhaps a father figure, or just someone to look up to because I did feel, no matter what he may or may not have been, he was an embodiment of love. I hoped that one day I too could somehow be an embodiment of love.

I was 19 when my mother decided to sell the house in Palmer Lake and move to Denver where she was working. I moved with her to go to college. When I was in high school, there was little thought about me going to college. All I wanted was to be finished with school, period. But when I realized that I could make this happen, I did. I had gotten myself set to attend Metro State University in Denver. The plan was to study finance. I simply wanted to make a lot of money. I was to get a fresh start to a new life. "The future was so bright, I had to wear shades." -Paraphrased from the 1986 song by Timbuk 3. That was my jam at the time...

Lori, my first girlfriend at the time lived in Colorado Springs and of course I had moved to Denver, which didn't help our relationship. We both had busy lives and were relegated to seeing each other on the weekends. It put an obvious strain on the relationship. But we continued forward for a while. The distance eventually took its toll and other realities like the age difference factored in to our eventual demise. She eventually concluded that this couldn't last as it was. She believed that I wasn't ready for what she was looking for because I was young. Plus, she was understandably concerned that I would meet someone else in Denver and break up with her. So, she broke up with me.

Perhaps on the surface, this is a relationship that was unlikely to last. Chances may have been slim as to our potential for a truly long-term relationship. But I only knew that I longed to be with her. It was a kind, warm, and passionate relationship! Ultimately, she did break up with me largely because of the age difference. She eventually wanted to marry. She thought I was too young and wouldn't be ready for marriage. Given I was 19, it's hard to say whether I might have been ready. While young, I did sincerely fall in love with her. I certainly didn't want to break-up. I felt we could go through anything to be together. However, I was feeling like I was starting to find my way with my life direction and maybe she was right. As a reflection of her integrity, she did the right thing for the right reasons. I'm glad to this day Lori, Connie, and Christy crossed my path!

The pain of that first heartbreak took me completely off guard. I had no idea a "broken heart" could hurt so much! Holy moly! I was overwhelmed by the pain. For all the pain I had been through previously in my life, the "broken heart" was the worst! I was completely "blown away" by utter intensity of it. Now I could actually empathize with all of those "heartbreak love songs" I used to love. When I listened to them, I really felt them and would sing along stronger than ever. I "totally got it"! It took a good year before I think I was basically "over it". Whew, that was intense!

Thankfully, despite some difficult days, I was able to stay inspired by looking forward to my new life. I was looking forward to the future!

My curiosity continued regarding Jesus. I continued to look for other sources of information about Jesus and Christianity. I started to study Roman history and the process and growth of Christianity in the Roman Empire. I had no wish to be disrespectful of the Bible but I wanted to know Jesus from accounts in the Bible as well as outside of the Bible. I also wanted to know what history said about him. During my studies, I learned about the Nicaean Council. The Nicaean Council was formed by the Roman Emperor Constantine in working with the early papacy which was becoming powerful. The purpose was to establish a standardized text for Christianity, a relatively new religion that had been persecuted in Rome but now was to serve as a means to save Constantine's legacy. That standardized text was to become the Canon, the predecessor to the Bible. Some say this is the birth of Roman

Catholicism or certainly a key part of perpetuating and empowering its growth and emergence.

The Nicaean Council chose what books, stories, or testimonials were to be included or not in the original Canon. It bothered me that any such group of humans, even if they are bishops or whatever they called themselves, had the right to craft the story into something that appeased them and their political agenda to expand their power. Much of this was to help reinforce Constantine's power which had been waning. The Roman Empire was beginning to fragment. This Council was to help open up a freedom to practice Christianity while putting off Rome's inevitable fall. Christianity had gone from a religion that was severely persecuted to becoming widely accepted.

Constantine took part in initially blending aspects of Roman Paganism with Roman Catholicism. The Bible and the story of God or Jesus is obviously of great importance and there is a big responsibility that comes with the telling and sharing such a story. It's my personal opinion the Nicaean Council failed at that. Politics and the agenda of the Roman Emperor Constantine and the council members were at work here, with each individual jockeying for position and power. Constantine's Roman political power was slipping while the papacy of the time was growing. It was significant for the papacy to become aligned with Rome as it was for Constantine to be aligned with the papacy. It helped to solidify Constantine's power before his death. With Rome's eventual fall, it opened the door for the papacy to grow in wealth and power. I'm certainly not suggesting my being an expert in religion or history but what I had learned made me see humanity's imprint on religion and the interpretation thereof.

In my personal opinion, none of the books or testimonials of Jesus should have been omitted. All the testimonials are important and part of that truth regarding Jesus and who and what he really was and what it means. I was feeling that the people should have been able to explore all available information and draw their own conclusions. But I could also see that clearly those in power didn't want that. Part of their power was in influencing something like beliefs. I also took issue with all the translations from Aramaic to Greek to English and all the other languages with which the Bible has been translated. Aspects, sometimes key aspects, of the meaning are left out or changed and some things get added, omitted, or altered. Having said that, I believe the Bible as it stands in all its current forms still has a lot of wisdom and should be studied. However, I had felt there was more to Jesus than the Bible despite what many devout Christians proclaimed. This is why I had also sought to also learn the perspective of historians plus take into consideration the opinions I was forming from what I had learned. Again, I wasn't intending to be disrespectful. I wanted to be sure to see past the dogma I was starting to recognize and understand for myself.

Eventually, I discovered some of the other accounts and historical beliefs about Jesus. Many came from the omitted testimonials from the Nicaean Council. There was a belief that Jesus had been married to Mary Magdalene. It's been suggested that they even had children. They then escaped execution to the south of France or perhaps to India. He is also believed by some to have traveled extensively before starting his ministry. There are those that believe that he may have been born with the name Issa. He traveled as far east as India and studied with the Hindus and Buddhists and traveled as far west as Greece. There are some reports that in those travels, he made it to England. There were those in ancient England who, during Jesus's life, believed in him. Considering the limitations of the availability of information and how slowly information traveled, it is amazing to think he had followers that far away during his lifetime especially if he didn't in fact travel there. Regardless, even then I understood that given the diversity of followers,

Jesus was a person for all people and all walks of life. I admired that and hoped to be able to emulate that quality. I felt there was something special about the person who was Jesus himself. I thought if I was to know him I would like to see him for the person he actually was including what he did as an embodiment of Christ (divine) consciousness. I'm know I'm not an expert in the life of Jesus Christ or the Bible but I know that Jesus was a person who was a friend to all types of people. He truly did not judge and had no ego. I believe and believed even then that if he were alive today he wouldn't just spend time with Catholics, Methodists, Mormons, or Christians in general. He would be reaching out to everyone in the world with love. He would be working to bridge the gaps that divide us to teach how to live peacefully together in the world without judgement. I appreciate much of what Jesus said. The message that is most telling to me is when he said, "You can do as I have done. In fact, you are capable of even greater..." – paraphrasing John 14:12. That tells me now as it did then that Jesus was not meant to be the exception, but rather the example. He was showing us all what we are capable of being and what the whole world could be. His message was never that we are "scum", "not worthy to be in his shadow", or "we can never be like him". He wanted to show us we are all capable of amazing things! That's a large part of what disillusioned me regarding organized religion. No, I'm not religious. No, I'm not a Christian because I walk all paths and have nothing but pure love and respect for the great teachers or "ascended masters" of many religions throughout history. I'm just as comfortable in a synagogue, mosque, temple, sweat lodge, Wiccan circle, scientific discussion etc. as I am in a church. But yes, I love Jesus Christ!

I could see clearly there were contradictions in the ways many Christians practiced and believed versus who I learned Jesus really was. I didn't often feel the love from those in organized religion. Organized religion was often judgement-based and in fear of that which is nothing resembling the love which is Christ consciousness. Plus there is the greed and exploitation by many religious bodies and churches of those who are blind and trusting of such entities. I did understand that this didn't encompass every Christian or church. But it was nonetheless prevalent in the religion. I can now see that it is prevalent in almost every religion or philosophy in the world, not just Christianity.

I also learned that much of the Biblical doctrine, especially the Old Testament, focused on the "do's and do nots" with respect only to physical acts like stealing, lying, et al. I was surprised at the violence, sex, betrayal and just the overall amount of "sin". But yet the New Testament, meant to embody the life and practice of Jesus, was based in love. Perhaps it was a transition in ways of thinking about God from an angry, vengeful God to a loving, peaceful God, at least in Christianity.

Regarding the idea of sin and especially the idea of believing or having faith, I had felt that one's intent and true feelings were what mattered most behind any given action. I had contemplated things like what if one person kills another in the defense of a loved one? Do we let the loved one be killed so we don't incur the sin of killing? Then have to live with that result, especially if you could have saved them? Which would be harder to live with? Would Jesus have allowed a loved one to be killed in order to remain without sin? Many Christians I talked to back then said Jesus would allow a loved one to be killed rather than kill and commit sin. I struggled mightily with that. Personally, I would protect a loved one rather than let them die at the hands of another due to my inaction. Of course, there is no way of knowing what the real Jesus would do in that situation. It seems to me to be a bigger sin, certainly the bigger regret, would be to allow someone, especially a loved one, to die when they could be saved even if it meant killing. Does the intention of protecting a person, innocent to a situation, change the dynamic of the act of killing? Is it still a sin? While I had far more questions than answers, it felt selfish to me to think of protecting my so-called soul from sin by allowing a loved one to die needlessly, especially if I could have protected them.

Conversely, regarding faith, I saw many people of faith doing their best to say and do the right things by their faith. They wanted to do right by Jesus/God. But their motivation for believing and practicing a religion was often out of the fear of God's wrath and/or the threat of going to Hell. So, if such a person did good by Jesus and God and was either sin-free or, the more likely possibility, repented and asked forgiveness, they would be rewarded with going to Heaven. They would want to be with God, Jesus, and their loved ones in Heaven for eternity. I could certainly understand such a wish. But doing good or being a good, loving person seemed to have little to do with love and more to do with fear. It was often belief motivated from the fear of God's reprisal including possibly being cast to Hell. That didn't feel like love to me.

I wanted to believe that if God was love and if Jesus was representative of love, it would be in what was in a person's heart that would matter most. I felt the action unto itself is just what's on the surface. It was the intent behind the action that mattered most.

I once asked a co-worker, a proclaimed born-again Christian, "Would a person who has led a loving life, even making a positive difference in the world, still go to Hell if they weren't religious in not having accepted Christ as their Lord and Savior?" He replied, "It doesn't matter how good you are. If you haven't accepted Jesus, you would go to Hell." Though I didn't say this because I didn't want to be disrespectful to my co-worker, my first thought was how can you be an authority on who is going to Heaven or Hell? Even in my naiveté for Christianity, I knew that the Bible talked about it not being our place to make such a judgement. That was exclusively meant for

God. I thought that a faith based in judgement which is a faith based in fear was not a true faith. That suggests that such a person basically wants to do right because they might "get in trouble" if they don't. It's like a dog not getting in the trash because the dog has been conditioned that to do so would meet with negative consequences. As such the dog avoids the trash. This is not a choice of an action based in loving intent, just the fear of punishment. It seemed to me based on what I was seeing that those who subscribed to a fear-based faith were the most judgmental. I believed that such a fear-based faith was the result of anger derived from the fearful insecurity of not really knowing or understanding aspects of spirituality or more to the point, having a fear of death. In their minds they aren't really sure they are going to Heaven or Hell...i.e., they lacked faith. I noticed a sense of protectiveness over their faith as though someone could take it from them. I've heard references to "my God" or "your God". My thought was, "Since when does anyone have possession over God?" Regardless of how any of us look at religion, many of these types of Christians become fanatical. They not only wanted to but needed to believe. It becomes everything for them to get everyone to agree perhaps because it helps them affirm their faith from the fear of dying and of Hell. But Love does not judge, cage, or bind. It sets you free!

There were times when I would witness a Christian in an argument with a "non-believer". Sometimes the argument would get emotional for both participants but almost always mostly the Christian. There were a few cases where I witnessed a Christian getting intensely angry! They would shout horrible things, even effectively telling the person they were arguing with things like "you're of the devil" and literally sentencing that person to Hell on the spot. I could understand, religious or not, they were still human and prone to anger especially when being verbally attacked for their faith or beliefs. But at the same time, it was their choice to put themselves out there. Regardless, that never "sat well" with me.

I would imagine what Jesus would do in such a situation. I thought, even if he was God's right-hand man so to speak, being at peace with total unconditional faith, he would stay calm and find a peaceful solution, even if to just "agree to disagree". Jesus would likely end up making friends with any such person. I had a hard time picturing him "force-feeding" his beliefs on people. He not only was a "fountain of wisdom and spirituality" but he would set an example in compassion, understanding, and patience in how he conducted himself. I feel, as a good teacher, he would have utilized every opportunity to speak his mind, especially in front of a large audience...just like he did during his life. In the back of my mind, I had gone through at least a small level of contemplation in becoming Christian. My thought was if I did, it had to be for the right reasons and I would have to find the right church. That never quite materialized. I still grappled with the concerns and questions I had no matter where I went. Did Jesus really require that I accept him as the one and only Lord and Savior as the only means to get into Heaven? And that's true, what happens if I simply live a life that benefits the world regardless of a belief in Jesus? It never felt quite right. I had a hard time believing Jesus would expect that. That feels egocentric. As mentioned, Jesus was without ego. I kept coming back to, "It's all about love!"

For many, it's natural to fear that which is not understood especially when it comes to people perceived as being different. I noticed that some of the most loving people were some of the most misunderstood, possibly including Jesus. But I knew many people, well outside of Christianity, who were genuinely good, loving people. Plus, they were open to befriending anyone from any walk of life they felt was a good person. I also felt strongly that good people come from all walks of life!

I also took issue with the fact that there is so much money being made in religion when so many people are hungry, homeless, and sick. I wondered if there was any one single major religious organization that wanted to change the world. Just like the Vatican, there are some immensely wealthy religious organizations. Look at some of those so-called "mega churches" here in the US. Many are worth millions upon millions of dollars. Most of those institutions donate a small percentage of donations received if any compared to what is retained. If a person is supposedly doing the work of helping people, I understand being comfortable but there is a point where the excesses of some are just a waste that could potentially benefit others.

I felt that the idea of Jesus' "miracles" like walking on water or changing water to wine take away from what he really lived and possibly died for. That was the message of love! I knew that for all I wasn't sure about regarding Jesus, the most important aspect of someone so prolific was being a representative of love. I had to wonder how Jesus would be perceived if the stories of his "miracles" weren't part of his story and message? His message of love should far outweigh whether or not he could walk on water or perform any of these so-called miracles. I distinctly recall thinking that love is the true miracle. Now the idea of breathing life into that which is dead is certainly significant and profound but it shouldn't take precedence to the message of love. If these miracles weren't a part of his story, would this most profound message of love have been overlooked or lost? It seems human to respond to physical acts of power, often missing the true power of something like love, even in religion. Because of this I remained torn, feeling frustrated.

No matter. To me, so much at the time was speculation and theory. I like to spend time contemplating and questioning. While I enjoyed pondering different perspectives on Jesus, the idea of him being married actually "humanized" him to me. I liked the idea that he may have been so extensively well-traveled to be a reflection of how worldly and open to different cultures and ideas he may really have been. This made him somehow more relatable to me. But there were still so many unknowns and possibilities. Given my questions and propensity still to focus on the physical senses, I was still reluctant to truly embrace religion and anything spiritual. But again, I still maintained the feeling that there had to be something more...

**

In the first few years after the move to Denver, my main interest was in making money. I started a mobile DJ business with a high-school friend named Ken. Kenny was a good person who could be positively hilarious! We always had fun! We played weddings, company parties, and had a summer long stint at a Denver hotel weekly barbeque event. I eventually started playing nightclubs. More to the point I was taking steps to become a stockbroker, in complement to studying finance in college. Over this period, I worked several part time jobs including bellhop, limo driving, and telemarketing. I was looking forward to a career in the financial sector. I simply wanted to make a lot of money. I never gave it a second thought. I never gave a thought as to how being in that field would feel regarding whether I would like the work and the environment. I thought money unto itself would be motivation enough. I thought it would be my ticket to a happy life. But this path in finance never felt good to me and I couldn't understand why. I was right where I thought I wanted to be but wasn't happy. I figured if I just stay the course I would somehow acclimate myself and I'll be fine. Maybe I just needed to get a little further along. While in college, I tested for the series 7 to become a stockbroker. I didn't get it on the first attempt, but I eventually passed. I spent a brief time as a stockbroker. At one time, I was working full-time, going to school close to full-time, and doing DJ gigs on the weekends. I was crazy busy living the life I thought I wanted to live. Yet at the age of 22, I was very confused, feeling empty, and lost even though my life had seemed good. How could I not be happy getting what "I thought" I wanted? It made no sense to me. I mean, who didn't want to be rich? I felt that regardless of my feeling somehow unfulfilled, it would all still work out. I was making good money, had a nice condo, and a new car. But there was an emptiness inside. This is a time when I took a step and reached out to Jesus. I prayed. Jesus seemed the most obvious and accessible to me, so I prayed to Jesus. At the time I didn't know who or what to reach out to. I felt I needed deeper answers and genuinely prayed for the first time in my life. I prayed to Jesus with all of my heart. I remember the first time I reached out I asked him to "please help me find a true meaning and purpose in life, and that I want to know what you know and see what you see."

I believe my prayers were answered, just not in any way, shape, or form of the way I thought. I did not realize the extent of the process I was to embark upon. I had hoped for a reasonably quick simple answer but that was not to be...

At this point in my life, my social life was pretty active too. I was mainly a "weekend party warrior". Most of the DJ gigs didn't go too late, so I often hit the clubs after. I liked to see live bands and go to dance clubs. I also liked meeting girls. I also enjoyed my party favors. I wasn't much of a drinker as I tended to be an angry drunk especially when I had too many. I was a marijuana smoker. That unto itself wasn't a big deal. But I did rather like dabbling in drugs like cocaine and speed especially if I was tired from the week and wanted a little "pick-me-up" to go out and party. I also tripped for the first time on acid. I really liked it. No matter, for all intents and purposes, I kept my priorities straight and life was good. Well, at least it appeared that way. I just stayed constantly busy convinced that's what I had to do.

It was December 7th, 1988. I was working a part-time call center night job when I got the call from my father that my mother had died. For some reason the authorities tracked down my Dad to give him the news rather than my brother or me. Though my mother had been experiencing some health issues, her passing was still unexpected. That day, I remember speaking to her at the end of her work day. It was about 10 minutes before she was to leave her office. We had a pleasant conversation about each other's day as we often did. And as we often did, we exchanged "I love you's" as we said goodbye. On her way to her car, she collapsed and died of a heart attack. She was already gone when the ambulance arrived. I must say I take comfort in knowing the last thing my mother and I said to each other was "I love you".

My mother had not been feeling well for about a year or so. She had, at times, been complaining of shortness of breath and chest pains. This was certainly cause for concern, but she had been seeing her doctor regularly. I felt confident she would be ok. He didn't seem concerned so there was nothing to be concerned about. In hindsight, he clearly didn't take her seriously. When she was symptomatic, he would have her take a few days off here and there "to get some rest". I think he prescribed her some medication though I don't remember what. At no point did he convey any sense of urgency or concern. He never suggested that she see any specialists and get any tests done. Initially, perhaps through some naiveté, I wanted to believe he was doing right by her as she did. There seemed to be no reason to be concerned.

My mother was very social and loved to get out and dance, bowl, play softball, and be generally active even though she was overweight. Over time, I began to see that she wasn't improving. The doctor wasn't helping. She was still complaining that she was having (heart-attack) symptoms. All the sudden, it hit me. I didn't have a good feeling about this. I confronted her with my thoughts that she needed to have her heart tested and examined. She was initially reluctant. There was some arguing, but she conceded. She had made an appointment herself, without the recommendation from her primary doctor, to see a cardiologist and have an EKG done. We had to be sure as to what was going on. My mother wasn't one to slow down for long. I believe it was two days before the scheduled appointment that she died.

It was almost 9 PM, as I recall, and I was about to get off work from the call center job. It had been a good night! The supervisor took me into her office saying I had a phone call. It was my Dad sobbing on the other end. Even though they had been divorced for years and were not particularly close since then, they did still love each other. They had known each other since they were teenagers. My Dad was almost unintelligible as he spoke. I knew before he said a word what had happened. My Dad, the blunt person that he is, just came out and simply said that she had died. A true friend, a person I loved and admired who truly loved me, someone who was always there for me, someone who always believed in me always seeing my best, and the person who was my rock and my mother had just died!

I was initially devastated! I completely broke down that night when I went to bed! I cried like I have never cried before! I couldn't stop sobbing for hours. Eventually I did fall asleep. I had an intensely lucid dream. I dreamt my mother and I were together. However, I was cognizant that she had just died. She was smiling, and we hugged. I begged her not to go and began to cry. She just said with a sense of concern but lovingly and sternly, "Never forget, no matter what happens, it's going to work out. Please don't forget, no matter what happens, you're going to be ok." I eagerly responded with, "ok, mom." She then looked me directly in the eyes and repeated herself at least a couple more times with a sense of urgency. She gave me one more big "mom" hug! I woke up with tears streaming down my face. I continued to cry at the reality that my mother was really gone. At the time, I wasn't sure if it was just my overflow of emotions or if my mother actually somehow came to me. It felt totally real! It's still one of my most powerful memories.

I will say, all of us family and friends certainly sent her off in style! I was the executor of her estate so I took care of all the arrangements. Everything went fast. Much of that time is a "blur" to me. I made most of the calls giving the news of my mother's death to everyone we knew. That was truly one of the hardest things I've ever done! There many reactions to the news. Some broke down, some couldn't believe it, some were just being concerned for my brother and me. For me it was heart-wrenching! But when we all got together for one more party for Miss Mike. Oh right, my mother's name was Michael. Her dad wanted a boy so bad that when she came out a girl, he still gave her a boy's name, Michael. "Miss Mike" became her nickname. All our family and friends came together in what was a beautiful experience mutual love and support!

I called around town to find a church to hold her funeral service. Since we weren't members of a church, it proved challenging. No one was willing to work with me. I called at least a dozen churches. There was very little compassion even shown given I had explained my mother just died. They didn't even offer recommendations. I was feeling discouraged because I wanted a church service. I felt my mother would have appreciated that. I kept looking. Eventually, I had found a wonderful pastor at a very nice Baptist church not far from downtown Denver. This pastor was quite the opposite of everyone else I had spoken to. He was compassionate, supportive, and was very happy to work it out with the church schedule for me to hold the service.

I wish I could remember the pastor's name. To this day, I'm grateful to him! The pastor did a wonderful job! The service was very heartfelt and I feel he really honored my mother considering he had never met her. There were at least 150 people in attendance. People came from all over town and from different parts of the country. I delivered her eulogy. Though I had tears in my eyes, I stayed focused. I read the "love chapter", Corinthians chapter 13, from the Bible. I felt it really exemplified my mother! She was a genuinely loving, caring person! Many people stepped up and spoke on her behalf. They were sharing some memories and what they loved about her. There were so many beautiful things said about her! It was amazing to me how many people really loved her and were touched by her in their lives. She was a very rare, special kind of a person! I realized even more as I was listening to the speeches how very blessed and grateful I'd been to have someone like her be such a key and integral part of my life! I was pleased and a bit relieved that everything worked out so well with the funeral service.

Following suit to what my mother said years before about wanting "to go out in style", I made point to do just that! There were plenty of tears at the funeral service, now it was time to celebrate the life a truly beautiful, loving person! After the service, everyone went to my mom's place. We proceeded to have a party that would properly represent my mother's fun, outgoing, and positive nature. We had a big DJ sound system set up. Did I mention she lived in an apartment in an apartment building? The service and wake were on a Saturday, a small concession to the other residents. The party started in the early evening and went into the early morning. My mom's apartment was "wall to wall" people and nobody left early. Everyone was talking, laughing, and reminiscing. We fired up the sound system and started playing my mom's and all our favorite music. People were now dancing. As the night wore on, we were pushing about 3 AM and the party was still going strong! The music was cranked up louder than at any point in the evening. The sound system was tapped. Everything had become deeply sentimental with the music. Like when we were younger, we all joined arm-in-arm and sang songs together. We capped it off with my mom's favorites "Come Sail Away" (live version of course) by Styx and "Magic Power" by Triumph. The sound system was peaked out and we were singing as loud as we could! "Magic Power" was the second of the songs. I'm pretty sure we shook the building. At the end of the song, we were cheering! As the cheering waned we and heard a knocking at the door. I answered it and it was an apartment manager. I said in my celebratory state of happiness, "Hi, come on in!" He politely smiled and explained that he couldn't. He then said, in the nicest possible way, "I know your mom just died..." He hesitates for a couple seconds and somewhat sheepishly says, "Uhh, would you mind keeping it down... at least a little?" In that moment, it "hit me" that we were in an apartment complex well past 3 AM. I had completely lost track of time. I responded with an apology. We decide to wrap up the party. Everything had worked so wonderfully! The wake was definitely another "one for the ages!" We definitely sent my mom off in really good style!!

**

In the span of time just before and after her death, I had a couple of rather difficult relationships that didn't work out well. In one case, it was a college girl who was playfully artistic. I got totally "played" but must say I should have known better than to pursue this even as young as I was. It wasn't a realistic situation. We met and got together over a Christmas break the year before my mother's passing. We got close fast. However, she was to go back to college out of state after her holiday break. But the passion was very intense. I took this to mean that we were supposed to be together even though our lives were clearly going in different directions. We thought to "sort of" stay together and look forward to the summer when she would be back. Needless to say, things got "complicated" during the time apart. She was seeing another guy at school. I didn't know this until she returned in the summer. Anyway, she was young too and it definitely wasn't time for either of us to be in a relationship. It took a while for me to understand that. At the time, it was just another hurt.

It wasn't long after the end of that last relationship before I was in another relationship. She was a smart, classy, beautiful girl. I cared about her deeply, but it was a hard relationship. She tended to be insecure about us having a future because she was sure I was going to leave her for someone "better" especially when I became financially successful. That bothered me. I wanted her to believe in me and us, but I wasn't sure how to handle it. It made me feel somehow cheap that she thought I was the kind of person who would do that. We were dating when my mom passed. The things that I found hard about our relationship coupled with losing my mother seemed make everything feel intensified. We had a bad night with a very avoidable argument and I walked out. I regrettably never spoke to her again after that. Now, given the relationship and its issues, it needed to end. However, I didn't handle the situation properly at all. Looking back, I wish I could have handled that in a more mature, respectful way. She deserved a better resolution than that. Both of us did. But everything that happened between us that night, coupled with my grieving, seemed to culminate. I "lost it" and left. All I knew is that I was completely emotionally overwhelmed and I had to be alone. She was a deep, wonderful person in many ways! Perhaps the hurts from her past played into her insecurities that impacted our relationship. While I now know I did my part in creating these experiences, at the time it was "fuel for the fire" for the grieving and pain in my life. No matter. She deserved better from me.

I was alone for long time after that. While all of this was going on, I was still missing my first love, Lori. Suffice it to say, I felt like I had been through an emotional acid bath, mulcher, grinder, smasher, explosion… yes, you get the point! I had a total and complete breakdown! I was feeling like I was metaphorically being stripped to the core. I had lost all sense of myself, my purpose, and direction. This was a process that would last for many years.

I would like to say I handled it well after my mother passed away, but that was simply not the case. I managed to give the illusion I was ok but over the ensuing months, I seriously "crashed and burned"! Yet none of my family or friends knew what was really going on with me. I knew that I was becoming something for which I was ashamed. After all, I had it in my head that I was just dabbling into some of these dark corners of life. This wasn't, after all, really me. I had thought I was going through some little phase that would somehow pass quickly. I could just go back to being me and this "little phase" could all go unnoticed. I led a sort of double life. As a result, I isolated myself and was alone with my pain. Within about a year, I deteriorated into a completely different person. Something truly dark came out of me. I fell deep into the dregs of life and myself. My life would continue to get much worse before it even began to get better. My life moving forward was going to be a much different experience than anything I had ever dreamed about or imagined.

There was around an 18-month span where I became addicted to cocaine, ate a lot of acid (LSD), and did a plethora of different drugs that included various forms of speed, meth, mescaline, quaaludes, and valium. During that process, I lost my home, my college education in dropping out of school, my car, and most of anything that was valuable to me. It culminated with me spending about two months living out of an old van that I had used to haul the DJ/sound gear. I was also selling and dealing these drugs. I came across some rather precarious and sometimes dangerous situations. I did and experienced things that I never thought possible for me. I never imagined I could do and see what I did. I was robbed, jumped, and beaten. I OD'd, was in fights, shot at, and saw some rather ugly things out on the streets. I did some ugly things myself that I never thought possible. I got a taste of what it's really like out on the streets and how dangerous or rather crazy I'm capable of being. Even Denver, especially in the late 80's, has some dangerous areas and people as I found out first hand. The side of drug culture I found myself in had shades of something out of a movie, though the reality with real people was completely different from fiction. It had become my life and was starkly real!

It certainly wasn't a time in my life I thought of as being particularly positive. My dreams had largely turned angry and violent. Both the anger and violence became forms of addiction unto themselves.

After falling behind on rent and other bills and because of all the things I was blowing my money on, I was evicted and became homeless. I did a lot of dumpster diving, looking for goods to sell at the flea market, though I had been dumpster diving for some time at that point. But no matter. The circumstances of my mother's death and this lowest low, having lost pretty much everything and my inability to understand and handle all my life's hardships, left me feeling completely broken inside. I sincerely once saw myself as a big money financier destined for great business success. I believed I was poised to make millions even billions. I was going to learn about life and the world by traveling. This was quite the contrast to the reality I found myself in, a drug addicted mess living life on the streets.

At the end of a rather tumultuous two years, I hit the lowest point of my life in every respect - physically, emotionally, mentally, and spiritually. This was a point of personal destitution. I had lost my career, my college education, my car, my home, and basically everything. I had become this cold, mean, angry person I didn't know was inside of me. But there it was. It was my reality. I remember thinking how far "off course" I gotten in my life. I seriously questioned if I had the strength to rebuild. I had ruined absolutely everything including me. I just felt so weak and so incredibly angry. Maybe Jesus didn't hear me when I prayed and maybe this demon I had felt a few years back was winning. And yes, I considered suicide! I thought long and hard about it many times. I couldn't imagine moving forward continuing to feel so appalled, guilty, ashamed, and worst of all, weak! I found these feelings unbearable! I came to truly hate myself! This was an incredibly intense time! I can now see what a powerful lesson it was. I discovered a lot about myself, most of which wasn't too pleasant. Everything I had become was a stark contrast with how I was raised and who I was growing up. I knew I had a bit of a temper, some anger, and hurt in me when I was younger, but this was so much more than that! I had a hard time "wrapping my mind around" how dark I was. I mean, I was truly dark and utterly putrid inside! This isn't the type of discovery anyone really wants to make about oneself. This was one of the most profound of my life experiences, and by far one of the most difficult to endure, accept, process, heal, and release!

I made the decision to quit using cocaine and the other drugs I was using except for weed. I will say the weed did help me to endure the cravings as I cleaned myself out, hoping to take the first steps towards rebuilding myself and my life. I continued to struggle with thoughts of suicide for some time. I felt like I had nothing inside to take these steps. It's like there was nothing there except raw unfettered anger. But I kept coming to the same conclusion, "I can't go out like this. Somehow, I have to do better. No matter how bad I feel and no matter how bad everything is I have to find a way to move forward." I started thinking in terms baby steps. You know, over time those baby steps really do add up.

With the help of my brother and my father, I made a move to Colorado Springs to get a fresh start. In the years that followed, though I had overcome most of my addictions, I had to come to terms with what I had done to myself and my life. I had to come to terms with everything I lost and the horrible things I did. I had a very difficult time being able to live with having cost myself what appeared to be a promising future while losing myself. I became consumed with having to come to terms with what had happened, the things I had done, and what I had done to others and myself. For years thereafter, I continued to relive all these bad memories in my mind. That made it even worse. I had hurt people and myself too many times and in too many ways. I couldn't get past the reality that there was something very dark, even wicked, within me. I was mired in guilt, shame, depression, and self-loathing. Those memories slowly sank in more and more as to just what I had done and the person I had become. The memories were unbearable. It seemed to be getting harder and harder to live with even with the passage of time. Then there was the thought, "what would my mother think?" I felt how disappointed and ashamed of me she would be. If she were alive, I wouldn't be able to look her in the eye. I couldn't bear living with these memories and feelings. I felt so broken inside and I had come to thoroughly and completely despise myself. I remember the feeling of how weak and completely unmotivated I felt. I decided I was undeserving of anything good given how extremely far removed from the person I thought I was and wanted to be. I didn't know how to find the strength to begin anew or even if I could or for that matter if I wanted to.

I continued to spend time contemplating suicide. At one point, I had even written a suicide letter. I knew exactly how I wanted to do die. But while I didn't have a clue how to move forward, I maintained wanting to find a way though these seemingly insurmountable challenges. Despite my sincerest doubts, I did my best to keep moving forward. I appreciated what my brother and Dad did in getting me a cheap little place to break away from the path I was on. However, while they knew the outlying story of my situation at the time, they didn't know the worst of it. Regardless, their assistance helped to keep me from giving up.

I made the move to Colorado Springs. I worked a couple of odd jobs including moving furniture for an auction house and as a retail sales person for a local record and CD store. Since I had been DJing since I was 16, I was hoping to find a way to DJ in a nightclub.

I was sitting on my front step by the street when this guy rode his bike by my place. I don't recall why he stopped but he did. His name was Luke, great guy, and we got to talking. It turns out he was a bartender for a nightclub/restaurant about a mile from where I was living. I promptly told him I was a DJ looking for work. Even without knowing me, he said he would help me out. He said he thought the club might be looking for a new DJ. He said he would put in a good word for me. We exchanged numbers and I thought, "We'll see what happens." As it turns out, I heard back from him. I got a meeting with the club's GM and he hired me for one night a week to start. Within a few months, I was working 3-4 nights per week including the weekends. I became immersed in the nightclub scene in Colorado Springs working for two clubs and dabbling in a few others. I became a pretty well-known DJ. I had a crazy, high energy sidekick named Herb. We became great friends! He was as honest and good-hearted a person as I have ever met! I loved that guy! He helped get the energy going, mainly on the weekends. Everyone liked him as he was a staple of the club. People loved seeing him dancing it up with all of his tassels and fun outfits. I even worked for a year as a commercial radio DJ. The DJing was a lot of fun and a big positive in my life! However, I was continuing to come to terms with what had happened and what I had done. I continued to struggle with suicidal thoughts. I had such hatred for myself that I hated what seemed like everything including God. So yes, at this point I came to believe in a "higher power" but not in a positive or loving way. I was mostly seeing dark.

I was as deep in my anger as I had ever been. No doubt I was in a deep depression. My temper was "off the charts"! I continued to think about my "demon". I wondered if it had somehow infiltrated me. In a way, I felt like maybe I had become a demon, given the anger and coldness I felt. I would think about suicide, but I continued thinking that "I don't want to go out like that." And I actually grew to find comfort in knowing suicide would always be an option. Besides, I felt like this so-called demon didn't want to deal with me "on the other side". There were many times I felt completely anxious and trapped. In those moments, knowing I had the choice to die surprisingly took the edge off my anxiety.

I thought if there is a demon inside of me coercing me, I wasn't going to give it the satisfaction. I'm "turning the tables". I thought, well hmm, if this demon thinks it's miserable now, let's see just how much it can take. I knew I could take a lot. I felt the only thing I was truly good at was being angry and hurting and destroying things, and sometimes people. I would destroy the demon, or if not, at least make it even more miserable than me. I knew I could be most proficient in doing that. However, it definitely wasn't the best decision. I dug myself deeper into my dark recesses within, to put it mildly.

Though I knew the road back, assuming I could make it, was still to be a long as in a year's long one, I eventually came to the decision to work my way through all the hard feelings I was experiencing and the mess I had made of my life. I decided that

I would start slowly putting my life back together, finding a new path. Again, baby steps. I began to search and explore the deeper truths, though there was a part of me still in a mindset of terrible anger. I had taken a small level of interest in science, mainly that of astronomy. I find it helped me to open my mind to new and different possibilities and expanded my mind to what was beyond life here on Earth. That grew into an interest in history, including learning more about different religions and philosophies.

In 1990, I had met a very special woman shortly after moving to Colorado Springs who changed my life! Her name was Micki. I had never known anyone who touched me so deeply and profoundly! We had a uniquely beautiful, amazing, deeply loving friendship! We were the best of friends for 12 years! Yet it ended as the most tragic experience of my life! I had never hurt like this before or since. She was one of the first people I had met and started to spend time with while I was living in Colorado Springs. I was immediately captivated by her combination of beauty, intellect, talent in numerous areas! She was highly intelligent and very deep. Back then she was explaining things that I've since come to understand through my NDE. This was, next to my NDE, the most intense period of my personal growth in my life!

Micki was also a multi-instrumentalist musician and vocalist, writer, painter, horse trainer and figure skater (before we met, she was an Olympic hopeful until an injury took her out of competition). I think that basically covers it. I don't think there was anything she couldn't do and do well. Her energy was like bathing in a warm spring in her unquenchably compassionate and loving nature. She always had a sense of "doing the right thing" and being sure to do her best to do it. I had never been so deeply touched by someone especially considering it was a time I didn't think I could be touched. She opened my mind in many ways. There were many times when we would talk and disagree for hours. We used to go on some long walks down a set of railroad tracks near where she lived. I had always thought I had good balance. But her having been an Olympic hopeful figure skater, she could walk on the track and never step off. I could go quite a long way without stepping off but would from time to time. Her balance was impeccable! She would just walk on the track and expound upon some rather deep ideals and have a great argument to support them. I would regularly disagree. But then I would regularly call her in the next day or two and say that I had thought about what she said. I was at least open to what she said and at times she had even changed my mind. I totally fell in love with her! For a time, it looked like we might become romantic. I was certainly hoping for that. We had a few moments early on, where we started to get close. But because of the very damaged space I was in, I essentially sabotaged it. Yes, it's the same refrain as high school but this was a whole different thing for whole different reasons. As mentioned, I had quite a temper. There were times I said mean things and became angrily argumentative. I apologized many times. She always forgave me. I learned, however, once the damage is done, there is no undoing it or taking it back no matter how bad you feel after the fact. Naturally, Micki didn't feel comfortable being romantically involved with me though she expressed how much she cared for me as a friend. I certainly didn't blame her at the time. I understood why she couldn't be romantically close to me. I wouldn't have recommended any girl be romantically close to me at that point. But the fact remained I had fallen in love with her and wanted so much to be with her. It was tremendously painful to be with her and not be able to kiss and hold her. I felt like we were supposed to be together and that I had failed her because I was so damaged and couldn't seem to bear the intimacy. The very thing that had always brought out the best out in me, that of falling in love, had brought out the worst. I knew I had no place in a romantic relationship with anyone. I would only find a way to hurt and disappoint a prospective partner and myself. However, the two of us continued to be the best of friends for the years to come. Whenever she needed me I was always there for her whether it was to keep her company, let her talk about anything she needed to, give her a hug, help her with tasks, or do just about anything she needed. I simply couldn't stop loving her!

She did meet someone she fell in love with. At first, he seemed to be the perfect guy. He seemed to be exactly what she had wanted and needed. I did initially have a very bad feeling about him. Then I second guessed myself. I thought it may be my hurt clouding my ability to see him for great guy he seemed to be. Micki really fell for him! As time went by, I even thought for a moment he could be someone I would like to emulate. Unfortunately, it wasn't too long before the guy she fell so hard for began to show his true colors. My original feeling proved to be correct. He became increasingly emotionally abusive to her. As a bystander watching this, I felt he was downright cruel! She was so wired to "love forever" that she couldn't and wouldn't break away from him. She was determined to give him every chance to work his issues out so they could finally be happy together. There was a pattern where he would be the "perfect boyfriend" for a while and then basically go stone cold on her. As she would begin to pull away, he would be that "perfect boyfriend" again and pull her right back in only to continue his pattern of emotional abuse. This went on for a couple of years before she finally broke up with him for good. She wanted so much to believe in him and he really took advantage of her love for him. I was close to her through that whole horrible relationship. Yes, I did shoulder some of the blame because I felt if I had been stronger and ready when I had the chance, maybe that terrible experience wouldn't have happened to her. She was quite depressed after that. It took her a long time for her to get over that relationship. But we continued to be the closest of friends! I can see now that was an experience that she may have had regardless of anything I did or didn't do.

Through the difficulties of the time, I serendipitously found myself with the opportunity to train in the martial arts. This proved to be a key turning point for me. Around '93 or '94, I discovered martial arts. I endeavored into my first martial art, that of Parker-style Kenpo Karate. I also got to train in Muay Thai.

I got into my first martial art of Parker Style Kenpo Karate because of a couple of friends of mine at the club where I DJ'd. The Parker Style Kenpo Karate is a fusion of northern Chinese Kung Fu with Japanese Kempo. It's denoted by the variation in the spelling. One friend was a Jazzercise instructor in addition to a Karate black belt and instructor. She approached me with a proposal to teach me Karate if I would help her by making some tapes for her Jazzercise class. Her husband would sometimes come to the club with her, but I didn't know him as well. It turns out he was also a black belt and instructor. He was a big guy who moved like a cat. I appreciated that he had extensive street fighting experience from when he was younger. He knew how adapt the Karate system to street fighting. I had the opportunity to train with the both of them. I really appreciated the "door" that was opened with respect to start of the path of martial arts. It proved to be an outlet I desperately needed for my anger.

During this time, I was also introduced to Muay Thai kickboxing. That's a style of kickboxing that not only uses punches and kicks, like Western kickboxing, but also elbows and knees. Strikes could also be below the waist. Fighters could also clench. The trainer who worked with me was a professional fighter himself. He once told me he thought that within 6 months to a year he could have me ready to turn me pro. He said I would have to work harder than I ever have in my life. But if I did, I could be a very competitive fighter, maybe a champion. The owner/sponsor of the team was a 135 lb. ISKA world champion at the time. So, I took what the instructor said to heart. The martial arts have been significant to my long and gradual transformation towards being a more peaceful person.

My temper was still pretty hot at this point. I still had a lot of anger, but the martial arts training was a fantastic outlet for that anger. It was the turning point of me starting to get control over myself and my anger. However, as I have said, progress was a long time in coming. Because of my temper, I did some (more) things, once again, for which I'm not proud. Because of my temper tantrums I broke a lot of things like doors, walls, TV's, stereo equipment, among many others. Plus, I still sometimes tended to get into fights. It wasn't often but definitely still way too much. I always rationalized to myself how I was in the right and the other person had it coming because they started it. I see now that there wasn't a single situation I couldn't have avoided if I so chose.

Not unlike my life in Denver, I still had a bit of double life because I didn't tell anyone close to me about the fights. I did my best to hide the damage to my place. With just a few exceptions, generally nobody knew that this sort of thing was happening. The same goes for my sex addiction. People knew I was always with girls but didn't know the extent of it and the level of my obsession with sex. My shame and guilt grew with each tantrum and each experience.

I had gotten into (non-sanctioned) fighting back then. Actually, much of it was "underground" groups. It was mostly when I lived in Colorado Springs and a few times when I eventually moved back to Denver. Back then there were no official sanctioning bodies in Colorado for boxing, kickboxing, or MMA (back then MMA had no sanctioning anywhere). Partly because of this, three or the first four UFC events were held in

Denver starting in 1993. At that time, the UFC held "no holds barred" bare-knuckle fighting events, as in there were basically no rules. This was before the evolution of modern MMA where fighters do now have rules. The early UFC fighters were specialists in a single art or discipline. They were generally either a striker or grappler. UFC or MMA fighters, in general, today often train in more than one discipline for both stand up and ground fighting. So, these early UFC events set out to show which martial arts style was the best since few of the arts were proficient both in striking and grappling. Around the time I started training, I rented the videos at the nearby video store so I could study the fights. I started to focus on the details of fighting. Karate is a stand-up or striking martial art. Though I had wrestled in high school, I found I had a far better knack for striking. I partook in a situation where it wasn't quite as crazy as the movie "Fight Club" but in a way, it was its own sort of fight club. There was usually a ring, we wore gloves, and we mostly used Muay Thai rules with take downs. No, it wasn't some secret group. Though not exactly advertised, it was open to anyone who wanted to fight. We had everything from the novice street fighter to some who fought at the pro level looking for chance to get experience and training. Though officiating was sometimes lax, fights that went to the ground were often stood back up and restarted unless there was clearly action happening. However, while there were a few fighters with a wrestling background, there were no serious ground fighters like in Brazilian Jiu Jitsu. But you still didn't want to be at the wrong end of a "ground and pound" by a wrestler. I fought quite a bit. Along with doing formal martial arts, I was participating in these fights on the side. This went a long way toward giving my anger a viable outlet.

By the time I was getting ready to move from Colorado Springs, I was becoming more the "nice guy" I used to be, at least outwardly in my day-to-day life. There was still a lot of dark inside me, but it wasn't manifesting nearly at the intensity or as often. I got into just a handful of fights after that. Now I can say, while I've helped to break up a few fights (having worked club/event security), I haven't been in a full-on physical confrontation for since around 2000 or 2001.

I do want to point out that those that I got into fights with on the streets weren't exactly innocent. While they may not have deserved what I did to them, they weren't victims. In most cases, I didn't instigate the fight, but I was quick to engage. On the streets, it's a sign of weakness not to respond quickly and to the point if someone shows you any disrespect. This stuck with me from my own time on the streets. It wasn't easy to just let go especially given the deep well of anger that was already there. But yes, again, I still could have avoided all these if I had so chosen. I've had situations when dealing with someone who was belligerent drunk, having a bad trip, or meth'd or coked out in which I felt I had to fight where I didn't necessarily have a choice. When such a person "loses it", it can make for a dangerous situation for anyone, including bystanders. Situations like that are hard to avoid when around people who are drunk or high on certain substances. Of course, a key has since been to not put myself in situations where such experiences are possible. "Preventative medicine…"

As a martial artist, I've done my share of sparring and fighting in controlled environments with people who are disciplined enough to get intense but not to escalate a fight into something other than a training exercise or competition. But it's different when the intent is to practice and train to fight versus being in fight where your opponent might kill you if given the chance.

It's interesting how even when I felt justified while in the moment I was in a fight, even in the cases I was dealing with someone who couldn't be rationalized with, I never felt good about it after the fact. While the initial rush of fighting felt good, soon after, when the rush wore off, I usually felt terrible all the way to the "pit of my gut". That's because deep down I knew I was in the wrong to have engaged or been in the situation in the first place.

**

In the last two summers I was in Colorado Springs, I had two experiences that a Native American Shaman might call vision quests. My dad, an avid four-wheeler, had some serious off-road trucks. We would drive on trails a couple of hours west of Pike Peak that required a four-wheeler and found a place that we came to affectionately call "Mushroom Mountain". We never knew the mountain's real name. Simply put, my dad and I had planned to take these days to find a beautiful place and trip on psilocybin mushrooms. It had been years since I had tripped on anything. I had no interest in LSD but I felt like I needed to do this. I had found a source that had some high-quality mushrooms from Oregon and bought some. Both experiences over both summers proved to be profound. They are still with me now.

My dad and I ate a sizeable amount of shrooms. Each of us really wanted an intense experience. We both got it! On both occasions, he would go hiking for many miles. He would be gone a good 7-8 hours each time, whereas I just became incredibly content to be wherever I was. I managed to get myself up on a rock overlooking a spectacular 180-degree mountain view. That was my spot the entire time which proved perfect for me. For the first time since I was a kid, I felt free and alive. For the first time ever, I felt "the pulse" of the Earth. I felt her life energy. I felt like I was tuned into every cloud, every breeze, every rustling of the trees. I could see nuances to colors I've never seen. Most importantly I felt love! It occurred to me that this is what it is supposed to feel like to live.

At one point on the second trip, literally and metaphorically, I had an experience that reflected the peaceful, resonant state I was in. I had laid back on the rock to look up into the sky. It was a gorgeous, mostly sunny day. I immediately noticed three Red-tailed hawks flying above me. Just then, one of the hawks started to fall. I thought, "What happened? I didn't hear anything." At that moment, the hawk spread its wings and swooshed on by not far above me. A second hawk and the third each did the same. They were taking turns falling out of the sky and stretching their wings and quickly flying past just above me. They were playing. I could feel it. I felt like I was up there flying and having fun playing with them. It was so liberating!

As I sat back up, one of the hawks landed right in front of me. I don't think the bird was more than about 6 feet from me. Talk about a "wow" moment! I had never been this close to a hawk before. He was surprisingly big up close. Wow, what a regal and magnificent creature! I felt completely at peace. The hawk stood there looking at me and me at the bird. He was moving its head and blinking as if we knew each other. I was so moved and felt so honored by this moment and being in the moment. After what seemed like about 5-10 minutes, he opened his wings and flew off around the mountain with the other two hawks. In that moment, I realized that this was how I wish I could feel all the time.

Going into the planning of these trips, I didn't have any sense that something like this would or could happen. I had trips on acid that were divine and expansive in the moment, but I would completely lose any feelings or visions and not be able to recall any semblance of sensation after the trip. On these two days on "Mushroom Mountain", something profound happened. This time around, the whole experience stayed with me. I could still feel a sense of what I experienced while tripping, including the thoughts and peaceful sensations. Knowing what a dark angry person I was, I found it curious that I could experience something so genuinely wondrous and peaceful!

While I had come a long way, there were still some more tough moments to come. Around the spring of 1996, I decided to move. Micki and I had not been speaking a whole lot. She had become rather withdrawn and had kept mostly to herself. In my inability to see the big picture and only see my hurt, I felt I had to escape Colorado Springs. I made an impulsive decision to move to Fort Collins with Scott, my brother. There appeared to be an opportunity in the music business for me. So I resigned from my long running DJ jobs I had in Colorado Springs and anything else I was doing. I didn't get into another club in the Springs which I should have, and found out later that once word got out I was no longer with my main club, all the other clubs' management were looking for me. I could have basically had my pick of clubs to DJ. However, I was still deeply in love with Micki. I realized I needed space if I was to ever have the chance to fall for someone else. I was feeling lonely though I had my share of "companionship" while in Colorado Springs. It just wasn't often particularly meaningful companionship. This was a big part of why I left Colorado Springs. I had a lot going for me there, though I really didn't appreciate it the way I could have in taking advantage of the many local opportunities in DJing and martial arts. Again, deep down, I felt undeserving of anything positive. I moved to Fort Collins which went rather poorly overall.

I was in Fort Collins for about a year and a half when I decided to move back to Denver in the summer of 1997. I had a fun job with good people by the time I left Fort Collins, but the pay was barely minimum wage. Ultimately, the move to Fort Collins wasn't a good decision. There was more negative about the experience than positive. While moving to Fort Collins was a regrettable decision, I did make some good friends and had some fun especially at my last job. It is a really nice town; it just wasn't where I belonged. On a whim, just before I moved, I called Micki. We had an awesome conversation. It was wonderful to talk with her! We began talking more often again. When I got to Denver we made a point to see each other more often too. She had been through another relationship that didn't work out. However, this one didn't have nearly the negative impact the first one did.

When I moved to Denver, I got into the live music scene and started DJing again. I first became a booking agent and publicist. I booked shows and did publicity all over the country. I also expanded into doing my own shows as well. I became a nightclub and concert promoter. I was blessed to work with some great Denver talent. I worked with a few artists out of NYC and LA among a few other places. I was blessed to promote and/or be a part of shows with artists like Bo Diddley, 311, Covenant, and others. Plus, I can say I did some of the best theme events in Denver featuring bands, DJs, fashion shows, performers, and dancers. I also DJ'd in a number of clubs. I also enjoyed and worked in different genres like Goth, Synth/Industrial, Fetish, Metal, and many forms of Electronica!

Even though there was a lot of darkness and an undercurrent of anger still inside of me, I was starting to feel a little bit better about myself and my life. I was a much more level person in how I conducted myself with people and situations. I wasn't getting into fights anymore. I had also stopped breaking things. Instead, I turned my anger in on myself. I thought that the anger was mine and my responsibility and no one else deserved to be at the brunt of it. That included inanimate objects as well. By turning my anger on myself because, well, I deserved it or, so I thought, I became brutally hard on myself. I became privately self-abusive. I would actually intentionally physically harm myself. I was especially mentally and emotionally self-abusive. I would completely demean and humiliate myself, seriously "raking myself over the coals" in my mind. In a way, I was punishing myself for all of things I didn't like about myself. Even though my drug addiction days were behind me, I still struggled with some of those memories. That self-abuse manifested into a horrible negative downward cycle that was pure poison to me. I really came to hate myself all over again. I even started allowing other people to take advantage of me and knowingly walk all over me. I believed I couldn't retaliate in any way. I let myself be a "door mat". I thought I deserved it because of all of the people I had hurt. With a few exceptions, that mentality became the norm for me for years. I became the opposite of what I was in becoming completely non-confrontational. It became hard to lash out at someone or even do something to stop a situation when I knew someone was taking advantage of me. It just piled up on me until this constant state of self-loathing and self-anger went right to the core. But what about my thoughts of suicide, you may wonder? These feelings were so bad and deeply ingrained that I believed I didn't even deserve suicide so as possibly to be relieved of my suffering. I thought I had to just stick life out no matter how I felt or how many times I might get the "raw end" of a situation. I should just be miserable as that is what I deserved. But despite that, I craved so much more! At times, I still dreamed about finding my life partner, the one who was the love of my life. At times, I still dreamed of an abundant life however fleeting. By now, I was quite convinced I was "the one" to set the example for positive change. So I held out hope and imagined I could yet salvage some semblance of a positive life. Still my darkness persisted in my guilt, shame, and ever persistent anger.

Micki and I started to get close again. I was finding myself finally feeling comfortable to be just friends. For the first time, I could talk to or see her and not be flooded with all those heavy feelings. I absolutely still loved her and would do anything for her! I had finally learned to just be friends with her without every "heart string" being pulled every moment I saw or thought of her. I appreciated her more at this time than I ever had!

However, her health was deteriorating from multiple car accidents in which she wasn't even driving. She also had fibromyalgia and TMJ, both which were getting worse. In 2002, she was in what was the worst of the car accidents. Micki was sitting the backseat of a car stopped because of an accident on the highway along with a passenger. She and this person were engaged in conversation. She was sitting somewhat sideways to better face this person with whom she was speaking. A car traveling at least 45 mph rear-ended them. Apparently someone didn't notice traffic was stopped until the last second. It caused injury to everyone involved and not to say what happened to the vehicles. That single accident seemed to accelerate and exacerbate her current health issues. She was now in immense pain and had difficulty moving. A visit to the doctor finalized a traumatic decision Micki felt she had to make. Her doctor took x-rays. He explained that her spine was leaking fluids in several places. It would need fusing, which is a major surgery. However, she would likely require several. This would leave her in even more pain than she was in and unable to walk. Micki had already, from her health condition and previous accidents, been through years of struggle managing her health and pain. This was the proverbial "straw that broke the camel's back"! She decided "enough was enough". Rather than live her life potentially "stoned" on pain pills and completely sedentary, she chose to leave this world. One night, she went to sleep and didn't wake up. She took her life!

A couple weeks prior to her death, she had told me about the doctor's appointment, the results, and her decision to die. At first, I completely panicked! I was initially furious that this would be an option and that she had to go and "freak me out". I went on to tell her, "If you go through with this, I won't remember you! I won't think about you ever again!" I hung up on her and "lost it", crying and yelling for about the next 15-20 minutes. It hit me that she was completely serious. I knew she would eventually do it. The hardest part was... I could actually understand. How could I expect someone who was so incredibly dynamic and loved so many activities like her horses and ice skating to stick out a life of pure sedentary misery? If my quality of life had become so compromised, how could those who loved me ask me to stay in such misery? I realized that this was the ultimate example of having to let go and say "goodbye" to someone you love!

We truly were the closest we had ever been! I went to see her and stay with her for the weekend at her home in Colorado Springs. We shared perhaps the most intimate and beautiful time together we ever had! She told me it would be any day now. We talked about our friendship and our lives together. She told me how much she had always loved me, still does, and always will! I didn't hesitate to expound upon how much I loved her! We explored what might have been if we had connected romantically all those years ago. She said that I was the one who was always there for her, no matter what, even when no one else was. She went so far as to apologize about how she understood how much it sometimes "tore me up" to do so. An apology certainly wasn't necessary, but it was appreciated! Needless to say, I was completely blown away and crushed at the same time because I knew it could never be. I stayed in contact with her each night thereafter until a few nights later when she passed.

I was and am still grateful for Micki's presence in my life! This experience was the full range of the deepest pain to the deepest love! In hindsight, I can see this experience was a key in preparing me for my NDE. Micki opened my mind to ways of thinking I would never have considered had I not known her, especially regarding spirituality and consciousness. I can't imagine where I might be without her influence in my life, especially during some of the most challenging times in my life. What an incredible blessing!

This, however, is when my dreams went silent.

**

The year that followed was without question the hardest of my life! To say I was heartbroken is a gross understatement! For all the people that I had known, loved, and lost including my mother, I had never grieved like this before. To lose someone I truly and deeply loved was already devastating unto itself, but to also realize that for all the regrets I was already carrying, thinking what Micki and I could have had by far was the biggest regret of all! That was the most profound missed opportunity I've ever had. However, this experience was on the both of us, not just me, despite my obvious mistakes and missteps. I had no idea how I was supposed to move past such a huge loss and regret. I had been working to maintain motivation, but this event completely killed it. The feelings were so powerfully painful! I was completely helpless to do anything about them. I genuinely had no control over this. I knew I had to go through this and hope I would find my way out at some point. I was able to continue to work and do my shows and such. But I was just going through the motions because I knew if I had totally let go, my life would be over. I remember waking up every day for that year sobbing. I would start my day listening to "Don't Give Up" by Peter Gabriel and Kate Bush and "Don't Cry" by Seal. I pulled myself together enough to take care of my business each day and then as soon as I was back home and alone I would cry myself to sleep. The feelings were so strong I literally couldn't help but cry any time I was alone. It was completely overwhelming! Thankfully I did reach a point where I finally started to feel something other than profound grieving and regret. After a brutally difficult year, I was beginning to feel a little bit more like myself again.

I was and am still grateful for Micki's place in my life! She was among the most beautiful of people or the most beautiful of souls I will ever know! She'll always be a part of me! She challenged my thoughts and my very beliefs, helping me to open my mind. I experienced one of my biggest life shifts with Micki in my life. She was an instrumental part of it. Though she has passed, she is still as much a part of me now as she was then. I will always love her! From time to time, I like to reflect back on some of those conversations while walking along the railroad tracks.

I was finally starting to feel healed inside of myself. I was also getting a grip on my anger and temper towards myself. Even though I wasn't officially training under a specific teacher or art at that time, I still practiced what I knew and worked out with several groups of martial artist friends. Unfortunately, I had gotten out of shape compared to what I was in the years before. But I was getting into better shape inside.

The summer of 2002, I feel like I won the martial art "Powerball"! It made my regret of not pursuing a professional career in Muay Thai (who knows, maybe I would have moved into MMA too) a bit more bearable. I was introduced to this crazy old Indonesian master who has since become a teacher, mentor, friend, and Uncle to me. I started training in the art of Kun Tao Serak Silat de Thouars (Kun Tao Silat or KTS for short) under the old master himself. I am an instructor. The Silat expression is Guru and Kun Tao or Chinese expression is Sifu. To coin a phrase, "I have found my art".

KTS is a fusion of Chinese Kun Tao and Indonesian Silat. Kun Tao is a distant relative of Shao Lin Kung Fu. It too, is also an animal martial art system, but the expressions are different. Hakka is a particular style or flavor of Kun Tao, possibly originally rooted in Mongolia, as "Uncle" suggests, many centuries ago. No one seems completely sure where it originates. Silat is primarily found in Indonesia and Malaysia. Given the 15,000 islands that make up Indonesia, there are many styles of Silat traveling from island to island. The primary styles of Silat we study are Serak (the de Thouars family martial art), Cimande, and a combination of Silat flavors from the many islands. Kun Tao Silat is a real world martial art. Like the Israeli Special Forces art of Krav Maga, it is meant for real life and battlefield situations. Something that may seem counter-intuitive about this art is that everything we do to break down the body can also be done to heal the body. As my teacher has said, "To be a true warrior, you must also be a healer."

The man who was and is the Grandmaster of the art is a world class Grandmaster named Willem de Thouars. He is known as "Uncle Bill" or just "Uncle". He is a phenomenally talented martial artist who has probably forgotten more than most of us will learn. He is simply "on a different level". He is an expert at the movement of energy, which the heart of KTS. I can't imagine that I could have learned anywhere else what I have learned from him. Uncle started training when he was 5. He was born in 1936, so you can do the math...The point is he is a rare and special martial artist who is veritable encyclopedia of martial arts and a true master!

Over the years, Uncle has trained in many styles of Kun Tao and Silat. He is also versed in the grappling arts like Judo, Jiu Jitsu, and including the islander style of East Javanese Silat, plus Western Boxing, European Fencing, Tai Chi, Qi Gong and other arts. It is a privilege to train under him or any of his teachers especially the seniors. He hand-selects all his students who are his teachers. While he wasn't the first to fuse together Kun Tao and Silat, it can be argued that he revolutionized it. He is also a key component to this information now being shared around the world and especially here in America. He regularly teaches seminars in places like Stockholm, Oslo, Moscow, Guadalajara, Boston, Truckee (in CA), and many other places.

His wife, whom we call "Auntie Joyce" or "Auntie" is a specialist in Cimande. Her father, Carl Dearns, taught Uncle the art of Cimande. She too is a master martial artist. She is known for her knife work with small blades, in particular, the karambit, a small bladed weapon with a curved edge. She is the family matriarch and also been a best friend and an "Auntie" to me!

This wonderful opportunity all started when a friend and fellow martial artist, told me about this relatively obscure martial art. I had never heard of it and was originally skeptical. I was craving the need to get back into some serious training. So I took him up on it. He had just started teaching as a Guru Muda (teacher in training) in this art. I thought to give it a shot. In some ways, I felt I was starting over. Much of what I was being shown seemed counter-intuitive to what I knew in my previous experience. This art was quite different than anything I had done or seen. I wasn't sure how long I would stay with it, but it was fun to train and even learn something different. I met some interesting people and some great martial artists a little bit before getting to meet Uncle for the first time.

Through my friend, I first was able to meet Uncle on a couple occasions. I participated in a couple of seminars he taught. So he saw me train a couple of times and spar once. I felt I wasn't at my best when Uncle watched me training. I was new to this art and I felt clumsy and awkward. I thought I had really embarrassed myself sparring as I felt like a shell of my former martial arts self. I wasn't acting and reacting the way I usually did. My timing was off. Also, my cardio wasn't the best. I think I did ok in my earlier sparring sessions. But then I had the good fortune of sparring with one of Uncle's senior teachers at the end of the sparring session. In other words, I was sparring one of the best! By then I was totally "gassed". It was terrible! The senior teacher essentially picked me apart. I saw everything coming and I knew what I wanted to do but my body just wasn't doing it. I got hit a lot. Don't get me wrong, this senior teacher was quite good. He was very quick and accurate. Regardless, I felt a little disappointed in myself that I couldn't at least be competitive.

There was an interesting turn of events. Some changes took place with two of the teachers splitting from Uncle and I had a bit of a falling out with one such teacher who kicked me out. Naturally, I "took it to heart" that my time in this art was over after only such a short time. Having gotten myself back into a training mindset, I started looking around for other training options. I started to look into Karate, Muay Thai, and Kung Fu schools. I started to think maybe I should go for something altogether different. I was in my mid 30's so the thought crossed my mind, "Do I compete?" and I thought that "window" had closed. Fighters don't start amateur or pro fighting this late in life. Of course, we know differently now, considering how many boxers and MMA fighters stay competitive into their 40's and sometimes 50's.

After about two weeks I received a phone call. It was Uncle Bill. I was naturally stunned. I didn't even know he had my phone number, let alone knew who I was. He was calling to tell me to show up on Sundays, his training day. He said, "Now I teach you real martial arts." I replied with a simple "yes, sir." I couldn't believe he actually saw something in me to want to invite me into this class full of really tough, talented martial artists! I was genuinely excited... and scared!

This is a special group of some of his best people and best martial artists I've ever met! For all that seemed to have gone wrong and for all my struggles, I felt this was a sign of things changing for the better. I was chosen to train directly under the Grand Master himself. I had regretted not pursuing a career in Muay Thai but in the long run this was the best thing that could happen to me as a martial artist. I've learned so many amazing things over the years from him and that amazing group of practitioners/teachers. I made some great friends who are all my "brothers and sisters"! This is a wonderful martial arts family! It's such a great honor to be a part of it! To this day, I'm so grateful for such a special gift! As I mentioned, we also learn about ways to heal. What I learned in this martial art, I believe, not only helped me to survive my NDE but also was a key part of my recovery. Hakka Kun Tao Silat de Thouars is my art for life!

During the course of the following years, I DJ'd fairly often, promoted or worked on countless shows, and was an MC of many events. I either put on or took part in live concert events. I also got involved in doing nightclub theme parties. These parties included DJs, bands, fashion shows, burlesque, go-go dancers, body painters, fire performers, and fetish performance. I also got into performing. I enjoyed performing with fire. Often, I would perform with a girl friend doing a fetish themed couple's burlesque. I had a lot of fun, made great friends, and have lots of wonderful memories! Along the way, I also worked in retail selling art, jewelry, and magazine ads. I even wrote some articles in a couple of entertainment zines based in Denver. I really met a lot of amazing and talented people from many genres of art and music. There were a lot of great times and great memories! In many ways, life was good!

Over this time, I had a genuine belief in God, though I was not based in religion. I still had love for Jesus but was also of the belief that those like The Buddha, Muhammad, Quan Yin, Lao Tzu, and Krishna were all essentially ascended masters and each had their place in history as the greatest teachers and some of the most enlightened souls to grace the Earth. I felt they were all more alike than different, despite appearances.

I made a point to watch more programming about religion, spirituality, and science. I was already interested in astronomy. I also developed an interest in the brain and the basic functions of the body. I also endeavored to learn about the Earth and how she was formed. A few years before my NDE, I discovered quantum theory. Though it didn't make much sense to me given its abstract nature, it still provided a sort of "wow" moment because it was so radically different than anything else within science. I found it mind-blowing to think that this is basically the true fabric of our classical, seemingly mechanistic reality. I appreciated and even embraced the unusual nature of it. There was at least some level of scientific evidence or at least some real consideration of the possibilities that the true nature of reality was nothing like we thought. For me, it was a whole new way to think about our overall reality.

In 2008, I started to write a book being inspired by these new ideas I was having. However, I only mustered up about six pages between this time and 2011 when I had my NDE. I was starting to perceive God differently. I was starting to recognize a certain connectivity in our relationship with God and vice versa. At the time the working title was "A Vision of God". I was starting to have a series of intermittent visions about the true nature of existence and, dare I say, God. But I kept getting hung up on all those hard feelings of guilt, shame, anger, and self-loathing. While I had healed and grown a lot, my dark feelings were still a huge struggle for me. I was finding myself becoming more and more sensitive especially with respect to empathy. I had always been a sensitive person, but my empathy was growing. As a result, my awareness of my past and impact of my actions was becoming more and more acute. It was intense! I got to where it was killing me inside all over again.

I had moments when I had thought that maybe I was to do something different than what I was doing. Perhaps it would be something that could have a positive impact at least on the people around me, especially those I cared about. Then memories of my past would settle in and I would think that I'm not someone who has the right or has any place to be some kind of example of anything somehow enlightened. Who was I to talk about God or anything spiritual? Besides, I was only realizing something that many had already been writing and talking about. I really didn't feel like I had anything to offer. As far as I was concerned, others who were far smarter, deeper, and simply better than me already had these topics covered. Besides, how would I get on such a path? I resolved myself that this life was "a wash". If I was meant for something different, well, "that ship not only sailed but it's probably somewhere on the bottom of the ocean". But still, I thought, perhaps I could salvage something positive from this life. I certainly wasn't getting any younger.

Even though I was many years removed from the worst part of my life and much of my life had improved, I still struggled inside. I was still promoting shows, DJing, and performing. I had some good jobs along the way and stayed busy. For a long time, I had hoped to get a shot at management in a nightclub. I certainly had the experience to be in charge of events and marketing in the right club. While I did some great shows and worked with great people, I had hoped I would have been further along that path. I had hoped for that high dollar position in a club. I came close a handful of times to no avail. But promotions and marketing were what I knew. I was good at it! I had hoped to find that club manager position for a long time, so I stuck with it.

I even had a wonderful girlfriend I loved very much, and I always will. There were many things about her and our relationship that I appreciated, not the least of which was how well we got along. We rarely argued. For the most part, it was rather peaceful. We met at a Goth club introduced by mutual friends. I got her phone number but didn't call her initially. I'm not sure why other than I was fairly active with dating...and somewhat easily distracted. However, I thought she was beautiful and classy when we met. I saw her at a picnic event a short time after. She jokingly poked fun at my not calling. Anyway, we got to talking which was nice. I felt like we "clicked". We ended up going out dancing that night. It was a blast! We started dating casually after that. Over time, as I got to know her, I grew to appreciate the person that she was. I really liked our chemistry. Eventually we got more serious and started a romantic relationship. We had a lot of fun and it was quite passionate! After five years it ended. It just seemed to run its course in a manner of speaking. Of course, like any break-up, it was hard for a little while and took time to heal. We didn't speak much for a few years, but we are friends now. We'll usually reach out on a birthday or the holidays. To me, she is one of the best, most beautiful women or rather people I have ever met! I do appreciate her and our experience!

In the year leading up to the fall, I felt like I was on an upswing. I was living in a place I liked with people who I considered "family". Some good things were happening with some great opportunities starting to materialize. I was still doing shows, DJing, and performing along with some side projects. A couple weeks before I fell, I finally scored an events management position with a new Denver club. It was a nice club with a stage and high-end sound and lights. There was also a big dance floor. It had everything I wanted to do the types of shows I was doing. Now I could have a "home base" and make the kind of living I wanted to make. Plus, I liked the ownership and other managers. I thought the club was really cool! It had a great vibe! I felt good that there was a big upside with it! I had waited for a long time to have this kind of an opportunity. Everything was looking most positive!

Yet somehow something still felt off. There was a part of me quietly gnawing at me that I should do something different. Again, but what?? How?? The reality was I felt I was deep into the path I was already on, having been on it for much of my adult life. I had been DJing since I was 16 and, at that point, promoting shows for 15 years. I felt like it would have been a major mistake to change up everything I had been working towards for so many years, especially given my earlier missed opportunities. The fact is I did like putting on shows. I can look back and say I put on or was a part of some great shows! It was a great feeling at the end of an event to be able to look back at the night, the big turn out, and the energy of people having fun! I kept telling myself that this is what I'm supposed to do. It was too late to think of doing something else, especially something that would require starting completely over. Yet through all the good happenings, I couldn't shake the feeling this still wasn't quite right. Since I had no real answers to understand or justify this feeling, I remained determined to stay my course.

About a week, maybe two, before my NDE, Canine, my roommate and close longtime friend, one of my brothers, asked me if I was alright. He said, "Even though everything seems good and you're keeping busy, you seem lost" and asked if I was ok. I told him that I didn't know, "but I'm starting to feel lost again like after I had just gotten cleaned up off the hard drugs all those years ago." I knew I still harbored those dark feelings inside. I was still hanging on to and struggling with some parts of my past. I considered myself still at odds over that. I wondered, was it that feeling of undeserving which lead me to make poor decisions and somehow sabotage situations? I thought if that was the case, I was moving past that phase and finally taking a potentially big step. I was grateful for the event management opportunity. I was very prepared to make the most of it! But no matter what, I couldn't get past the sense of something being off. I just didn't know what the heck to do with it.

It had been quite a life at this point with what turned out to be a lot of awesomeness but also some incredibly difficult experiences. Like many people, I had my regrets. I wished I could have made some different decisions and done quite a few things differently. I had learned an immense amount about myself. I was good at being unabashedly honest with myself, sometimes to my detriment. I certainly did hurt people and I was hurt. I had seen a great deal with my life across a pretty wide spectrum of emotions and experiences. I had a wealth of information at my disposal. In a way, it seemed that I was maybe for the first time in my adult life starting to establish and define myself as a person. It felt important to truly learn from my experiences and actually apply them to the person that I wanted to be and how I wanted to live. I knew I wanted to be and felt I could be a better person, and be abundant!

Unfortunately, yet interestingly, while I enjoyed getting lost in thought, I had no dreams per se. I didn't daydream or fantasize about anything. That had been the case since Micki died. That was something too with which I still struggled. There was a sense of emptiness when I thought about dreams. I seldom remembered my dreams when I slept. Strangely, I barely even noticed.

I was starting to get a sense of the idea of the law of attraction in films like "What the Bleep" and "The Secret". Although I recognized that it isn't simple or cut and dry, I could see that there were many variables involved. Simply put, I was starting to see how I could have attracted and created all my experiences. This in turn influenced and became the intent behind my decisions perpetuating the energy I was putting out to the universe. I was recognizing the cycles in which I was stuck. We've all heard the expression, "You get back what you put out" or "What goes around comes around" or even "You reap what you sow". I felt like the living embodiment of that. I did however understand that was essentially true for all of us. Therefore, I made the decision to take full responsibility for everything in my life! It sure did make my perception of myself and my life much simpler. In a way, it made everything informationally feel more accessible and understandable.

I thought I would just continue as I was and promote great shows. I thought my life would all work out. If I just "stayed the course", any feelings of being lost would in time subside. I didn't know what else to do. Based on what I felt I was looking at with my life, I thought this was the right thing to do.

Then the totally unexpected happened...The dreaming of the ultimate dream!

3

The Most Incredible Day

On August 10th, 2011, my life took a thoroughly unexpected turn. It's true - I fell out of a tree. My life as I knew it had come to an end. I had a certain… "experiment with gravity". Let me start by saying that I found gravity to be most effective! Hey, all Newton did was have an apple fall out of a tree on his head. I actually fell out of a tree on my head. No, I'm clearly not Newton, or Einstein for that matter, but I do have some ideas about gravity. I'll get into that in Book 3.

Ok, here's what got me into that tree to begin with. As a long time martial artist and instructor, climbing has been a hobby and source of cross training. It is great for building core strength and balance. I often climbed rocks, mountain sides, and trees. I was in a tree in a park in Northglenn, CO, just north of Denver, having stopped there on the way home from an early morning training session at the home studio of a senior instructor with Uncle. This weekly session started as always at 7 AM every Sunday. Because I'm not a morning person plus I often worked events Saturday evening into early Sunday morning, I would usually be tired after class and would normally go home to sleep once the adrenaline and endorphin rush of the intense training wore off. But on this particular Sunday, I found myself with a lot of energy and felt like getting some more exercise. I stopped by a park nearby my home at the time and went on about a 3-mile run. Still feeling energized, I decided to climb a tree. I had climbed this tree many times before. But this time two branches broke under me. I have a recollection of the moment where I knew I was definitely falling and going to hit the ground. As I began to fall, I remember "playing the moment down" in my mind, thinking this wouldn't be a big deal. I thought, "I'll be ok. I got this!" and "Nothing but a flesh wound" ala Monty Python's "The Holy Grail". I fell unobstructed, hitting head first on to a concrete bike path. The police report lists the fall at 26 feet. This was quite the dramatic turn of events after the rather uplifting morning training session with Uncle and my nice peaceful run.

It was chilly overcast spring day. On my run I think I may have passed one or maybe two people. There happened to be a couple of high school girls passing through the otherwise empty park. I'm estimating these girls were 50-75 yards away. By chance, they happened to be looking my way when I fell. If it wasn't for them, I would have died on that concrete path due to internal bleeding from a badly punctured lung. The girls immediately called the authorities. When the first responders arrived, I was apparently still conscious as per the first responder report. I have a vague, spotty recollection of this. I just remember thinking, "I want to go home."

Sometime in those first few minutes after the fall, I went in to deep shock and lapsed into a coma. I was rushed to the hospital. When I was first brought to the hospital, I had massive bleeding on the brain in three places. I also contracted pneumonia, had a heart rate of over 150 beats per minute, and had a badly punctured lung that kept filling with blood. I was placed on a mechanical lung. I went into respiratory crash multiple times over the first few days. Whenever my lungs would fill with blood, I stopped breathing and would have to be resuscitated. While I don't believe I flatlined, I was near death. It was uncertain whether I would survive my injuries. In addition, I was unable to eat or drink for ten days, losing significant weight.

At a recent appointment with a doctor who had seen me from the beginning commented, we reflected on my time in the hospital, that "There were a number of times we thought we were going to lose you!" The thought at the time, while still comatose, was that even if I did survive, my quality of life would likely be compromised both mentally and physically. I was in a coma for five days and had broken 20 bones. In addition to my ribs, my pelvis was broken in four places. I cracked five vertebrae in my neck and upper back, broke my fibula, and essentially destroyed my elbow. Interestingly, the only damage to my head, besides thoroughly scrambling my brain, was a broken orbital bone. One of the senior instructors in my art has since joked, "Well, we don't have to wonder how hard Rex's head is." Fortunately, the bleeding on the brain stopped on its own as it was not operable. I was able to recover most of my faculties and memories.

Although I don't remember much of the first week or so after waking up from the coma, I have lots of stories I could tell about my month in the hospital. That includes what it was like to have my head slowly "come back online" after coming out of the coma. It was a gradual process. I understand that I was rather volatile at first. For a time after waking up, I didn't know what had happened or even that I was injured. Yes, despite the fact that I couldn't get up, despite that I was so weak that I could barely move, and despite having external fixators on my hips and left arm, I had no idea what was happening. All I knew is that I wanted to leave this place that felt like a distant dream and nobody would let me. I couldn't understand why. That upset me and so I acted out. I was told that I said some mean things to the hospital staff. My memories of this time after the coma are spotty, mostly just a series of disjointed images.

The worst of it may have been when, although I don't remember this, a couple days after I woke up I somehow defied physics (20 broken bones, blah, blah, blah) and managed to get myself up out of the bed. I pulled out all my tubes and IV's, and even my catheter! Yes, I do cringe at the thought of that. I attempted to walk out of the hospital. A couple of the hospital staffers restrained me and forcibly put me back to bed. Apparently, I resisted, which seems a bit laughable. With 20 broken bones and after five days in a coma I doubt it was much of fight. Frankly, I'm surprised I could even stand.

The first time I remember getting up to walk was the single most physically difficult and painful moment I have ever experienced! I could barely move and didn't go far because I was so weak and in tremendously immense or immensely tremendous pain! The point is, it flippin' hurt! So, imagining myself getting to my feet shortly after waking up from a coma, let alone offering any form of resistance, is amazing to me! I knew I was a little bit crazy but that is ridiculous. Needless to say, I was put back to bed and placed in restraints for a couple days as insurance I wouldn't try to do it again. However, I did try again in a couple days removed from the restraints. I remember the second time in vivid detail. It was late night, early morning. It took everything I had to slide to the edge of the bed. Once again, I just wanted out. I was fortuitously intercepted by a nurse presumably doing her rounds. She scolded me, threatened the restraints, and helped me get moved over on the bed and laid down. By the second partial attempt, I was starting to become at least semi-cognizant of the fact that I had fallen from the tree and was badly injured. I apologized and managed to convince the nurse that I wouldn't do it again. Thankfully I wasn't put in restraints this time.

My brother, Scott, was with me every day. As I have been told by him, family, and friends who came to visit, I seemed very "scattered" mentally for much of my time in the hospital. I remember that focusing was rather difficult. I tended to be "all over the place" when trying to converse. I was unable to stay on any given subject or focus on any given person for long. My mind would just wander from "place to place" or from thought to thought. Although, as I had become more aware of the circumstances, one of the first things I did was make sure I could remember my martial arts forms. I ran all the forms that I know through my head. I was very relieved to be able to do that. Many of the memories of my time in hospital are still a bit fragmented especially early on.

I also had some very detailed hallucinations soon after waking up, some of which I remember as clearly as the memories of my hospital stay. In some ways they reminded me of some of my acid trips; however, they were far more painful. One of my most vivid hallucinations in the hospital consisted of my believing I was in Los Angeles. In my career as a night club promoter, I had held an annual Halloween event called the Vampire's Ball for ten straight years. It was a fun, performance-heavy theatrical style event with DJ's and some years with bands. I had a hallucination that I had gone to LA to meet with club owners about doing the event in a club there. I imagined that I met with two different club owners and their staffs. I discussed the concept, themes, performers, DJ's, marketing, and pretty much every aspect of what I planned to do with the event. But the reality of it was that I, of course, I never left the hospital. Within the hospital, I was taken by wheelchair to two different areas to be given tests. I was actually "having these meetings" on the LA event with members of the hospital staff. They got to hear my whole pitch about the event while running the tests. Ben, one of my wonderful physical therapists, was with me. He told me later, when I was more cognizant, that I sounded like I really knew what I was talking about. He told me that if he owned a club he would hire me. I remember that hallucination rather vividly, but in the context of a hallucination.

While my memories of my stay in the hospital are spotty, I can differentiate between the hallucinations, no matter how vivid, and the images of being in the hospital perhaps because of my experience with hallucinogens.

There's something I still find interesting about the way my brain was working. A cognitive therapist would visit me every day and put me through a series of tests. Naturally, she had diagnosed my difficulty with focusing and short-term memory loss. She would also leave me with homework to do before our next visit. Most of the time I would forget to do it and we would do it together. Each day she would visit, the first questions she would ask were, "What day of the week is it? What is the date? What year is it?" Initially, I struggled with all three questions. I can remember that when she asked, the information just wasn't in my brain. I would totally draw a blank. Eventually, I was able to answer the first two questions, but I struggled on the third, the year. After I gave my answers (which for a while were guesses), the therapist would tell me the correct answers. My sister-in-law, Elizabeth, told me that at one point I was guessing different years in the 1980's. My guesses eventually made it into the 2000's. For nearly the last week I was in the hospital, I said 2007 every day. For some reason, I got stuck on that year. I'm still not sure why. A few of my friends who were privy to that still jokingly ask me what year it is. Naturally, I answer, "2007, of course."

I've always been able to be my own objective observer. Even back in my drug days, a big part of the reason I was able to always "come back" from an acid trip is because no matter how much I took, what I was experiencing, or how intense the experience, I always knew I was tripping. I could tell what images and sounds were the result of the drug. That objective and lucid part of me could even tell how I was acting around others. I did the same thing in the hospital, especially after I became a bit more cognizant after waking up from the coma. I could tell that I wasn't completely lucid and was easily distracted. I felt like I was seeing through other people's eyes. Though much like being in the peaks of an acid trip, I found I could do nothing about it in the moment. In a way I knew I would have to "ride it out" like an 8-hour acid trip. But in becoming more lucid I also knew I could take certain actions to help perpetuate the healing process. This personal observational objectivity helped as I learned to start helping myself.

I was blessed to have had a couple of excellent physical therapists while in the hospital! One of the physical therapists at the hospital, Janey, seemed to take a bit of chance in how she coerced me to get up to walk the first time. I think it was about a week after I woke up from the coma. I was still in a quite scattered and angry mental space. I was just beginning to comprehend what had happened and where I was. Even with all the pain meds, I was in incredible pain! Plus, I had metal fixators on my left arm and pelvis. My left elbow had been basically destroyed in the fall and was essentially completely dislocated. There was little left intact to relocate it. When the doctors tried to put it back together, they had a tough time. Most of the joint to hold the elbow together was damaged. The doctors put metal rods in my lower arm through my ulna bone and upper arm through my humerus bone with a metal joint-like hinge to hold the elbow joint together. With my pelvis broken in four places, I had a four-inch screw inserted in my right side and external metal rods screwed into my hip bones on both sides. They were held together with a bar shaped like the front of a boat. This is not to mention my many other broken bones. I was also weakened by the fact that my swallow function didn't work. Anything I swallowed went straight to my lungs. I went ten days with no food or water. I was being fed intravenously. Plus, even after I was able to start to swallow correctly, it took a few more days before I could eat a whole meal. I lost a lot of weight. I'm 6'4" and dropped to the high 140's from about 195 lbs. Needless to say I was very weak, in pain, and in no mood to move anywhere! However, nowadays, it is deemed imperative that a trauma patient start moving as soon as possible. I was expected to get up and walk. Yeah right!! But due to some clever and somewhat disconcerting psychology, Janey got me to get up to walk.

Technically, hospital staffers, doctors included, can't actually make someone do something they don't want to do even if it's in their best interest. Janey had come by my room a couple of times to get me to walk. I had abruptly and angrily refused to get up and sent her off.   Well, I clearly underestimated Janey. This one day she would not be deterred! She stood in the doorway to my room and asked if I was ready to get up. I would only have to walk a few steps. Thoroughly annoyed, I rudely said "No, now leave!" She then said to me, "You know I have some time before my next patient. It's okay if you don't want to get up but I'm going to stand here and just stare at you until I have to leave unless you get up and walk just a few steps. If you do that, I'll leave." I was watching TV at the time. I told her to "get out!" and continued watching TV trying my best to ignore her. She basically said, "That's fine. If you're alright with me staring at you while you watch TV, then go right ahead." I tried. I really tried. I think I lasted maybe a minute. I really couldn't stand to have her in my doorway staring at me like that. I'll never forget this curly brown-haired woman with these beady eyes and wire-rimmed glasses just leering at me. It really got under my skin! I very rudely yelled at her to f***ing leave now! She grinned and responded "I'm not going anywhere until I have to leave for my next patient or you get up." She shrugged, smirked, did a pfft, and continued in a rather smug, nonchalant way, "Besides, what are you going to do about it?"

I thought, holy s**t, did she really just say that to me?? I about lost my mind! I was so furious at the audacity of such a statement! I couldn't believe she said that to me! I think I may have blown real steam out of my ears. I didn't say anything initially. I sat quietly thinking to myself, "Do you have any idea what I am trained to do?" But then my next thought was a very disheartening, "Oh yeah, I can't do any of it! Grrrrrr!" Finally, I said, "Fine!" and realized she was right. I slid myself to the edge of the bed with every ounce of strength I had. She placed a walker in front me and I got up. It truly was the pinnacle of physical pain! I have never been in physical pain like this, period! The broken ribs, elbow, et al were rough but not compared to my pelvis. I walked about twenty feet moving a few inches at a time with very small steps. It was all I could do to maintain my balance. Janey stayed right next to me. I made it a short distance outside of the door of my room. At this point, I looked at Janey and said, "I really can't go any further." She promptly said, "See I told you, you could do it! Now that you know you can do it, I'll see you tomorrow and we'll do it again. Now let's get you back to bed." I smiled and calmly said, "Yes ma'am."...Well done, Janey, well done!

That was my turning point. From that time forward, I became a model patient determined to do whatever I had to do to heal! As much as that experience with Janey absolutely infuriated me, she was right! She "had my number" and knew what she was doing. She totally did the right thing! For that I'm grateful! I came to like Janey. She became one of my favorite people at the hospital! Both physical therapists Janey and Ben were awesome!

Over the last few days of my hospital stay, I was able to take significant steps in being able to focus and be more mentally functional. That sense of personal objectivity in observing myself helped. I could see that I was struggling to focus. I came to see how I was forgetting to do the homework from the cognitive therapist. I began to put my focus on being in the moment and taking things one at a time. In a way, I slowed myself down to make conscious decisions in each moment. I made a conscious point to focus on my brother, a medical staffer, a friend, my homework, and especially every conversation. On the next to last day in the hospital, the cognitive therapist had lunch with me. She wanted to get a closer observation on how I was doing. We had a nice conversation. At the end of the conversation, she explained that she initially thought that I would need months or maybe years of therapy, but she had noticed a quick change with me in that last week. She said after talking with me over lunch that she was going to release me from therapy. She explained that she has never seen such a dramatic turnaround in her years as a therapist. She was great, but I was so happy to move on!

On the day I was released, as a testament to my stubbornness and how determined I became to heal, I walked out of the hospital. This was a month after I fell. Yes, I had to use a cane and I was moving slowly, but I walked out on my own. It was just a couple weeks after that memorable conversation with Janey when I could barely move. I knew the road to recovery would be long and hard, but I felt confident I could persevere.

All the while I was coming around in the last couple weeks of my hospital stay, I realized something was different. I knew something happened when I was comatose. At times, I felt a sense of love and peace like I have never known. I also felt a sense of "being" like never before. At this point, these were just sensations. I considered whether this was caused by the medications that I was on, but I generally didn't like the way they made me feel. So I knew it wasn't that. All I knew is that I had a lot to think about. This felt profound! I just didn't understand how or why.

One of the most important things I learned is how blessed I really was. I had a steady stream of visitors almost every day over the last couple weeks I was hospitalized. Scott, took care of contacting many of the people that I knew to inform them about what had happened. He waited for about a week after I woke up before he let anyone come and visit with me. As I mentioned, I wasn't in such good shape mentally at first. Scott didn't want my friends to see me like that. Thank you to Scott and Elizabeth! You both stepped up big time! Thank you, cousin Chris, for flying in from Michigan! Thank you to Uncle and my entire martial arts family! Thank you, my long-time brothers Canine and Doug! Your support was and is appreciated! Thank you Kaya, John R., to my club family in the Electronic, Goth, and Metal scenes! Thank you to my Dad, Shirl, John B., and my Colorado Springs family! You all rock! And many thanks to all the amazing friends who spent time with me while in the hospital! I was and still am blown away that all the wonderful people who took the time to come and visit! I'm absolutely grateful to every one of you! I had not considered what I had with all the special people in my life before I fell. I could have died that day never truly knowing and getting to appreciate this important part of my life. I'm also grateful that I was able to live to not only see it but also appreciate it!

The broken bones have healed and I can now walk normally. It took nearly two years to get through my subsequent surgeries on my pelvis, shoulder, and elbow. There were many hours of therapy. I went through an out-patient program with every step of the healing process. Lori, my out-patient therapist, was wonderful and very diligent in working with me. I generally visited her three times per week to do a series of exercises and TENS treatments. She also gave me specific sets of exercises and movements to do daily on my own. I was given a device for my elbow to help increase range of motion post-surgery. When I had it on my arm I joked that I felt like "The Robot" from "Lost in Space". Lori was just about as determined as I was to get my body working. My elbow was the biggest challenge. She had told me that she had only seen one patient in her years as a therapist whose elbow was worse than mine. I know she was "just doing her job" but she was awesome! She was an integral part of my healing! While it may seem counterintuitive, my martial art of Kun Tao Silat was a key part of my therapy. I was very restricted with what I could do, especially the first year following the fall. I would do my stretching and forms. A number of the exercises included elements of Tai Chi and Qi Gong that are a part of the art. Essentially, I did as much as my body would let me do. By doing all those movements in addition to what I was doing with my therapist (including the "homework" she gave me), I was successful in my recovery. I treated my therapy like training, especially integrating my martial arts into it.

After everything, I still feel like me. A part of me is still the "me" that I was before the fall. But, at the same time, I'm different. Being on the verge of death and knowing how close I came to dying gave me a deep sense of my mortality. I could see how fragile life hangs in the balance. This whole experience has been as humbling as it has been enlightening. I have found a deep peace with the experience and more than that, with myself. I released all my anger, depression, guilt, and shame. I was able to let go of all the negativity I was carrying. I have a genuine and sincere love for life and for all parts of this whole experience! I have new realizations quite regularly and am seeing a slow evolution of my life in a completely new direction.

Not only did I survive but I exceeded virtually every medical expectation with my recovery. I believe I was blessed to have the best in both Western and Eastern healing! All my Western doctors were supportive of the Eastern healing practices my friends performed on me. This has been and continues to be a truly major event in my life! Yes, this experience was a mixed blessing. I still have some issues with which to be mindful with respect to my head, elbow, and back. There are still long-term health issues, the most significant from my traumatic brain injury. I'm largely dealing with headaches, brain fog, short term memory loss, fatigue, and a serious lack of directional sense. However, I'm constantly challenging myself so those symptoms are improving, though there's still a long way to go. On the other hand, something in my mind changed. Something opened up in my mind. I see life and existence more clearly now than ever. Most importantly, I feel I am, for the first time, truly "waking up" and seeing beyond this "brick and mortar" reality. I feel comfortable thinking in the abstract. I am able to make sense of and visualize many scientific and spiritual subjects in way I never could before. I will touch upon some of these ideas soon. I now live my life with love, purpose, and making dreams come true!

Here's what happened within the ultimate dream and a little bit of what I have learned thus far...

4

Dreaming the Ultimate Dream

As I get into expressing my visions on the esoterics of my experience, I will present this information as though it is fact because, to me, it is. From my perspective, this information is the direct result of my personal experience. This experience is more real to me than anything else in my life. Love is the basis of this experience. However, the experience, ideas, beliefs, and life mission shared in this book aren't meant to preach or tell anyone what to do or think. While what I am going to share is no longer a belief to me, I do realize much of it cannot yet be proven or disproven. These are ideas or perhaps at the best maybe even theories. Some of what I'll delve into is being explored in sciences like theoretical physics, quantum theory, and cosmology. My goal is to offer insights from what was, to me, a profound experience. For you, the reader, these new-found revelations may be treated as "food for thought" or something to ponder. As my friend, Trina, likes to say when presenting, "If it resonates keep it, if not then throw it out. That information is not for you, at least not at this time." After all, we can all offer one another guidance and ideas, but we still must find our own way. We must decide what it all means and how to apply it towards how we choose to live our lives.

Intuition, empathy, and imagination are not some random aberrations of evolution. These qualities evolved for a reason. They are a part of us physiologically and spiritually. We have this capacity already within. It becomes a matter of tapping into it in a moment of time. I have found that if something resonates or simply feels right, chances are it is right. After all, consciousness, love, life, and mind (not just referring to the function of the brain) are inherent within us to the core. But although we experience them, there is no way to prove or disprove any of them as of now. How do we quantify an experience? On a scale of 1-10 or something like that? Does such a scale or measurement reflect the nuances of an experience and that which makes it unique? Explaining it, let alone proving it beyond knowing you're experiencing it is a difficult challenge. Yet it is our intuition, empathy, and imagination that give "color" to our conscious experiences in love, life, and mind.

For as intense as my physical, emotional, and mental experience was, there was something even more intense, profound, and life changing than anything I endured regarding the healing process. Something happened that was more real than any part of this whole experience or for that matter any part of my life!

My experience while near death was on the one hand simple but at the same time infinitely deep. While in the coma - perhaps it was during a respiratory crash - I had a moment of pure lucidity. It was all-encompassing of every fiber of my existence. This was the single clearest, most profound, influential moment of my life! It was more real to me even than the reality of sitting here writing this book. I distinctly remember being in the light and darkness all at once. I could be either or both with a thought. Space/time as we know it was irrelevant.

This actual experience unto itself felt like a moment. While in that unconscious state, I had no sense of my physical body, but I was still me. I knew I was on verge of death, but I also knew I wasn't going to die. While the experience may have been unconscious, the visual realization of the near-death moment - like remembering a dream - was completely conscious. The lucidity of the dream was far more resolute than anything I've experienced in this reality. It was 4K high definition times at least a million. It was essentially an ultra-brilliant dream, but as the ultimate reality.

I was experiencing my own pure being but as pure being itself. I saw a reflection of myself as the whole of the universal mind at the "heart" of being. I saw the whole of reality as a reflection of this source or divine mind. Within it in that moment were the contents of every aspect of reality.

Imagine for a moment if the information of this source being could be quantified as a form of singularity. Imagine all of space/time but as separate aspects of the same construct. Imagine the expanse of the universe - whatever it may really entail - all at once. Imagine the expanse of time - whatever that may really entail - past, present, and future all at once. Think in terms of the information of the entire universe as particle-sized singularity just before the proposed "Big Bang".

Imagine the entirety of all of possibility and probability - in other words, imagine the realization of the concepts of multiple realities and parallel universes. This may include universes where different versions of us are having different variations on our experience to universes that are completely different forms of reality that may not include a "version" of us to universes so abstract that we can't begin to fathom them let alone share a form of experience. Imagine this is all a part of that same singularity.

With that, imagine infinite dimensions all at once. What could that mean? This could span various combinations of interdimensional experiential consciousness. The potential for conscious experience is infinite across these infinite dimensions of matter, thought, and being.

For a moment, it was all me. For a moment, I was this source being, source mind, and source consciousness. I will go so far as to say, this source was what we may call God. This was me in my purist form as pure source being itself. This is something we all share at the core our being and is inherent just by the nature of our existence. There is a Mayan expression, "In Lak'ech", which basically translates in to "I am you, you are me". It was a salutation used as an expression of how we are each an extension of each other's being and consciousness. From this experience, I have a true sense of this expression of complete connectivity especially on the deepest divine source level.

I had no sense of my body or anything physical. I didn't actually visualize anything. However, no matter how I focused, underlying the experience, I could still feel the divine permeating every part of me and every part of the all...which was somehow still me. I could feel this is the core part of each of us and everything in existence that is infinite and eternal. Though I have a visual expression with respect to explaining the memory of the experience, it was simply more closely described as an experience that I profoundly felt. I didn't "go" anywhere or even "do" anything. For a lack of a better way to describe or explain it, in a moment, I just simply "was" the all of everything. I was the source of consciousness or that of the divine or God.

I felt that I was being shown something that I was to share with as many people as possible. As I was only just coming to understand, this "something" was already a part of me. I felt light in the conscious source "fabric" of love, life, and mind. But especially, there was love with an absolute pure unfettered clarity. This "light" was more than just light. It was the essence that is at the source of all aspects of the experiential part of being, whether light or dark. I felt this underlying source to be in essence "fueling" or "breathing life" into the source experiential consciousness, aka the unified field in quantum theory. This was basically the source of love, spirit (life), and mind in a state of potential (vs. kinetic, the action of being in in an experience in a moment) energy and simply in the purest state of each. This is completely fundamental within everything and all of us. There was no form of "verbal" communication per se. It was for me more of a thought process. This thought process came from the deepest part of me, my soul. I see it now as abstract visualizations but with a specific signature frequency, that of love. It's like I already knew, like having a sense of total divine knowledge, in my observation of this deepest of dreams. It was all completely instantaneous and felt like nothing more than a moment, but there was an eternity in that moment.

I had an intention to explore. Have you ever been in a dream while sleeping and you knew you were dreaming? That's how it felt but in the most brilliant way. When you're dreaming, it's easy to want to explore and do things you can't necessarily experience in the physical "brick and mortar" reality. Perhaps you have wanted to fly in a dream or breathe under water, like I mentioned earlier? Knowing you're in a dream state, you are able to do pretty much anything you want. You can do or be anything you can imagine in the dream state. Being aware I was effectively in a space beyond the physical existence, like an ultra-clear super-vivid dream, I wanted to experience this space. As I thought to explore, I simply knew I had what I needed.

I thought about "crossing over" and allowing myself to die. But I simply knew I was to come back. I wasn't given a choice per se. At least in terms of my mortal, ego-based self, I had no choice. I knew I was to come back to continue living this life. I felt a powerful sense of wanting to share this experience and what it means with as many people as possible. Now this is hard to explain and perhaps really grasp, but I did feel other forms of consciousness in that near-death state. Like I had said, this was all my pure being yet pure being itself. In other words, I felt many different forms of what could be considered individual forms of consciousness within this singular consciousness, but it was all an extension of me as I was the extension of all of these different forms of consciousness. I was in effect simply somehow thinking or visualizing direct thought within myself as a small piece of the source mind. I could feel the spirits of my mother, Micki, Jeff, and so on. But, I was still the person that I am in our "arrow of time" reality construct. Again, this source mind or more to the point "I" was all one with the infinity of existence including my loved ones! In effect, I was the infinity of existence just as I was this divine source! In the experience of being near death, I had the sense that, for just a moment, I knew everything as I was everything yet somehow I was nothing other than love, spirit, and mind. This divine source was or rather is the source of "the all" as well as being that part of me that is the source. In other words, for a moment I was the divine source of not only my own pure being but pure being itself. I was my soul. I was God! A truth that resides in each one of us!

So on one hand, when I had initially woken up from the coma, I was totally lost. But on the other hand, as I was "coming back online", I knew I had this powerful underlying sense of love with these images floating around in my mind. I remember mentioning to a couple of people, while in the hospital, that somehow, I experienced something while comatose. At the time I certainly wasn't sure what it was, let alone the extent of it. I just had a sense that something had happened. It was something that, like a seed, took root and became stronger with the images continuing to become clearer over time.

Despite these feelings, it still took a couple of months before I actually realized I had a near death experience. I had been watching NDE videos and contemplating whether something like this happened to me. By this time, the feelings and images were starting to become clearer. During an appointment with one of my doctors who was there when I was first brought into the hospital, it occurred to me to ask that question: did he consider what I had gone through to be a near death experience? Without hesitation he said, "Yes." It was quite the epiphany when I realized I had actually had a near death experience!

Given my new-found realization, I really started to focus on the experience itself. I found it surprisingly easy for me to go into that space of divine being and further process this information. Even now, when reflecting or meditating on it, I feel I can go in a deep state of lucid dreaming, whether waking or sleeping, and have experiences beyond our corporeal existence. But it's always as a form of the divine. I'm still processing and coming to understand this information now. This will most certainly be a lifelong process of growth and understanding as the person I truly am as "Rex".

Because of the nature of the communication, given the sense that I could feel that this divinity was me in my pure form, there was no resistance to what I had experienced. Simply put, that's just the way it was and what was meant to be. Therefore, it was natural to accept. And well, here I am...

Perhaps the most notable change that came with this love that has awoken inside me is how crazy sensitive I've become. I feel everything so much more. While watching a movie with Scott and Elizabeth shortly after my release from the hospital, there was a commercial break. A "Maxwell House" commercial came on. It was one of those pseudo-romantic ones. I believe it featured a couple on a beach with a lighthouse in the background as the sun came up. They were toasting their morning coffee together in sharing a touching moment. I, as quietly as possible, started crying, moved by the perceived beauty of this "Maxwell House" moment. Hey, it was bloody romantic! Scott looked at me and asked, "Are you crying?" I quite reluctantly and grudgingly answered, "Yes," and left it at that. To this day, I'm easily moved by even the cheesiest of scenes in commercials, TV shows, or movies. That's not to say how moved I can be when it's a real-life experience. It takes little for to me cry, as much as I prefer not to admit that. However, these tears reflect many things, both happy and sad. I had been on a spiritual path for many years before this whole crazy experience. I even attempted to start writing a book prior to my NDE, but to little avail. I believed it was much too late in my life to shift, plus I had no clue with the "how or what" to shift. Feelings of awakening were fleeting. Many old hard feelings and temptations were always getting in the way. Prior to the fall, I had practiced extensive meditation especially with respect to my martial arts studies to help maintain some balance and "vision". Now after my "experiment with gravity", I feel totally awake, no longer carrying the burdens of my past. I'm always feeling that same sense of the light of love, life, and mind I felt while near death. I feel I have been reborn. I still meditate but now much of that time is spent exploring what the divine is and what the NDE means with respect to my newfound visions and applying it to my life. No matter what is happening in my current life, these feelings are always permeating every part of me. For me, this is absolute truth!

Let's explore the divine dream...

5

Love, Spirit, Mind, and Consciousness

Perhaps the most impactful part of the moments near-death was the incredible pure love I felt! But it wasn't just love, it felt alive as the source of life itself, and intelligent. But it's not intelligence as we think of it. It was a purely lucid intelligence or pure mind. All of this are the qualities of source consciousness, which is the source of everything experiential. These qualities are all the most basic or fundamental properties of the source being. They are different qualities but the same. They are the "heart" of our experience and who and what we truly are. This is something that goes well beyond our physical or classical reality. Yes, this gets deep into the quantum or etheric depths, whichever you prefer. Many experts in the quantum field largely believe they are studying lifeless little packets of energy that have unusual properties. These levels of thought and existence are the movement and perpetuation of the most profound parts of our living experience. I heard a Hindu expression that says, "it's all consciousness". I'll say that it's all love, spirit, mind, and consciousness!

LOVE

So, what is love? We all know the statement "God is love". But

God is also spirit, mind, and consciousness in its purest essence. Consciousness is the embodiment of love, spirit, and mind as it is core source of all that is, including everything that exists in the universe including the universe itself. Consciousness produces matter NOT the other way around. It is through the fire and passion of love that spirit and mind arise out of consciousness. As such comes creation itself in all its intricacies and vastness.

Love is the highest, purest state of fulfillment. Love is the deepest level of connection, a soul connection, especially relating to our experience. For us to walk the path of love in our lives may mean many things depending on where we are on that path versus what could be called our highest path. Love does what's best for a situation by taking steps toward the highest level of fulfillment, contentment, or potential. It is the basis for the experience of our most powerful feelings and emotions.

The love of physical or superficial things is a form of infatuation or obsession, some more extreme than others. This is based in the ego and self-satisfaction because it is about personal gratification instead of doing what's best for a given situation or a person one purportedly loves. In obsession rather than love, the focus is on "how they make me feel when I'm with them." This may be taken to the point of subscribing oneself to believing, "I am nothing without you." Such a person becomes addicted to these feelings to the point of violence should they lose the object of their infatuation. On no uncertain terms is this love. This is an example of pure selfish ego in the extreme. A person that loves thinks about the ways to bring something positive to another's life. This person's happiness becomes part of our happiness.

In some cases, the infatuation changes or comes to an end. An example is when people, who are romantically involved, talk about "falling out of love". This is basically saying that the person you were in the relationship with no longer serves you. A person in this space will break up or leave the other. That is not an example of true love but a passing infatuation. I'm not suggesting it's "good or bad", but it isn't love. This includes any kind of relationship or friendship.

Some people have a hard time differentiating between infatuation and love. The emotions associated with infatuation and obsession can be most powerful. It can potentially become all-consuming, thereby being a distraction from the other important things in our lives like time with our loved ones, taking care of ourselves, our careers, or anything else that may be of importance in life. If you're in any form of relationship with someone you believe you love, look and see if it is draining, stressing, and leaving you feeling stuck with no way out. If so, chances are you're infatuated or obsessed. Or perhaps someone is infatuated and obsessed with you and being a catalyst to your stress and potential for distraction.

Obsession is not always a bad thing as long as it seen for what it is and kept in perspective. Preferably it should not applied to relationships. For example, I do have some obsessive-compulsive tendencies myself. Perhaps my biggest obsession is martial arts. I live it and breathe it every moment of my life. I do have a certain obsession for it. But, given my nature, it is a positive outlet and a positive obsession for me. It brings me good health, a sharper more disciplined mind, and deeper understanding of the body and how energy moves given the art I'm in. If you have an obsessive or addictive nature, be honest and aware of it and focus it into positive things like being healthy, climbing that mountain, going on your dream trip. Any number of things can be positives. But obsession doesn't have a place in a truly loving, healthy relationship. Infatuation is selfish, confining, and conditional. True love sets you free and has no conditions or limits in the love. It just "is"... no matter what!

While love is the impetus for the most profound,

compassionate, and beautiful of experiences, that is typically an end result of a journey or a fresh beginning of one. Love is about what's best for an overall experience. That may entail experiencing hardship before experiencing the beauty. If one commits to living a truly loving life in finding their highest path, life may become a veritable "Hell" before it finally synchronizes and all the pieces fall into place to create something more "Heavenly". Love can completely strip you down to build you up as the proverbial "phoenix rising up out of the ashes". To quote Steve Miller, "You've got go through Hell before you get to Heaven." For some of us, like me, that is quite true. Especially for most of my adult life, I was a great distance from being my best in love and walking that personal highest path. When I asked Jesus to show me what he knows when I was 22, I can see in hindsight that something shifted in my life at that moment. I had no idea of the hardships to come. But now I understand it was all part of a purging process in healing and releasing the darkness within me. This eventually culminated with my NDE. Love, or perhaps angel or spirit guidance which is love, led me to the extremes it did because it took all the extreme difficulties in my life just to reach me. Now I feel like I'm better learning to act in loving ways, whether in tough or soft love.

This whole, often disappointing and difficult, life experience, arriving at the point of my NDE, was all done in love. I know that sounds almost ridiculous. While hard to see in the moment, it was what was best for me to finally "wake up" and find my way in this life. As I understand it now, there were energy dynamics behind it. If I am to be honest with myself in looking at the "big picture" of my life, I accept that all the apparent missteps and mistakes led to the life that is growing now. It seems contrarian, but while it may have seemed to be negative, it was what was best for me during those times in my life given the space I was in. This is not to say that I now actually "know what Jesus knows", but my NDE has opened the door for an experience and understanding of a higher consciousness and a more loving way to live my life. While in the past, my intention and actions weren't often loving, the experience of pure consciousness was because my desire to "see and know" had always been genuine.

I started my life in a light place. Eventually that broke down. I experienced great darkness within myself and parts of my life in both my actions and the situations I attracted and indirectly created (though I certainly didn't understand that then). Case in point, this emergent property of divine source, love, did what was best for me and my situation considering where I was inside by guiding me, over the course of many years, to the beautiful place that I'm in now. During extended periods of time, love was brutal but at other times, especially now, soft and nurturing. As part of the overall synchronicity, the experience of love in my life has changed as I have changed from within.

When it comes to people and relationships, love can mean many things. Sometimes it is the binding to connect people for a lifetime. If the love is true, it is still experienced whether the person or people are in your life or not. "Love is forever" even if the experience isn't. For as amazing as a relationship may be, the relationship itself may not be meant to last forever even though the love does. Sometimes the loving thing or the best thing to do is to say, "Goodbye". It may rip your heart out to do so but you will heal in the continuation of evolving your path of the experience of love. While it's sometimes hard to endure, love is about doing what is best at all times. Even when we don't understand why something must hurt, if we trust and have faith, we will always come to understand growing and learning in the process.

In defining love, a neurologist, psychologist, sociologist or other "experts" on the subject may reference chemical reactions and synaptic patterns in the brain, pheromones, and other physical traits that generate the sensations of love thus creating the experience in our brain. With respect to the attraction that exists with a prospective couple, there are a number of processes taking place within brain and body that can be measured and analyzed. There is love between family members, close friends, and family pets. There is also, for many people, a love of our planet, living creatures in general, and of course God. While scientists explore the effects of love on us physiologically, psychologically and socially, it can be overlooked to delve into the internal, even esoteric, side of love, that part of love rooted in the imagination of the source consciousness.

I would suggest that love is the result of God consciousness or the "force" of God. This is where love itself imparts an inner strength, wisdom, and ultimate fulfillment in a person's life. Naturally, the brain will act accordingly in reflecting the effects of this underlying loving force or energy in the contents of this mechanistic process. It's all connected and working together. It stands to reason the physiology of the brain would reflect that. But the center of the will driving one's intent is not centered in the brain or the even heart. They are primary transceivers of the experience, but not where love originates. Love originates in quantum depths transcending all of creation and existence from beyond the source field of consciousness or unified field just as we all originate within the experience of simply being in love, spirit, and mind.

Emotions and thoughts are frequency, just as is all energy. Although we don't have a means of measuring these frequencies of energy yet, every emotion and every thought has its own frequency or combination of frequencies not unlike a musical chord. The thoughts we choose to experience have everything to do our perception of reality. It is through our deepest pure intent at the source of thought that we manifest our reality. Whether we realize it or not, we are all doing it all the time. It can range from a musical chord being played out of tune like a musical train wreck to the same chord being perfectly resonant and in tune, resulting in total harmony and synchronicity.

When everything is in sync, it's like a band playing a song or an entire symphony orchestra playing a complex symphonic piece of music. These emotional frequencies have power and impact our reality. They can be felt internally through our source depths to our deepest feelings to the emotions we experience throughout the course of a single day. They are played out through our actions including the choices we make rooted in our intent based in these inner depths. When everything is in sync and resonating with the love of the divine source, we can do anything and be anything. This is an example of the quote, "Love can move mountains". With the love frequency, "If you can imagine it, you can do it!" It's possible to manifest any dream.

Anger has a different frequency than love. To me, it is a fear response. Anything that taps into our fight or flight instinct is what I term a fear response. It's isolationist, furthering the illusion of separation. It draws a person out of and away from their deeper being. It puts someone into a space and a perception that is stuck believing that the five senses represent the totality of reality. In this vibrational space, the experience and the belief system will represent a potentially materialist, separatist, and survivalist mentality. This an example of an experience that sees only one's physical self and then everything else instead of seeing the self expanding into everything else.

Opening the door to the soul and putting these intentions and emotional frequencies of energy out to the universe will influence what you get back in your life based on how it mixes or harmonizes with the love resonance at the source. Your soul's frequency can be in tune or out of tune.

Reality will respond accordingly and energies will be carried out in the way things come together and play out in the experience. We've all heard of the "law of attraction" or the expressions, "what goes around comes around" or "you get out what you put in". If you live your life with the perception of anger, events and circumstances in your life will take place so as to reinforce and perpetuate that anger in some fashion. The same is true for any emotion or set of emotions that reflect a perception of reality. That perception is reinforced through actions which could be the start of negative patterns. This is not a static or simple "black or white", "1's and 0's" thing. There are many variables at play here with what one is projecting outward and what one is subsequently attracting in one's life.

The negative or low vibrational emotional states are supported in one's perception and beliefs. This often leaves one ensconced and consumed in the external aspects of life. It becomes easy to fall into believing that this is all there is to life while giving little or no consideration to anything loving or spiritual beyond that which is physically tangible. This despite the fact we all feel love in one form or another. There isn't a lot known or a lot of scientific evidence beyond measuring and studying the physiological processed involved. Science isn't yet sure where love originates. Science doesn't really have a definition for love beyond explaining the mechanistic functions of the brain. But for most, love is the most real, most powerful part of our experience!

Knowledge can be found through study, wisdom can be found though experience, and enlightenment can be found through love. But love is more than just an emotion or a set of physiological factors. It is a purely fundamental force working as parts of mind and spirit that is the "heart" of consciousness. Scientists may not yet have a way to measure this force, have physics for it, or have discovered particles that drive this force, but it is undeniably real! Perhaps this force is somehow hidden in those complex physics equations? Regardless, this force of love is the key to the "opening the doorway" of our soul, the soul of God. It's the doorway to realizing and beginning to understand our inherent connection to this divine source and each other. It is the force that drives the vibration and frequency of existence. It is the will to "be", but not just to exist. Like Shakespeare said, "To be or not to be, that is the question." Love is the will to flourish in the most complete most fulfilled state of being! Within us, love perpetuates an innate sense to grow, bond, and thrive. It inspires us to do and experience amazing things while being at our personal best! In other words, love is about learning to fulfill our potential in becoming everything we were meant to be and sharing it!

The universal being grows and evolves seeking the experience of its highest, most fulfilled state of being in love. This is true even in the moment-by-moment perspective. Love is the ultimate underlying connection of everything in creation, including the universe. Love is the connection of all that is. The force of love perpetuates the evolution and experience of the "all" on the universal or multi-universal scale throughout the entirety of the space/time experience.

For us humans, what does it mean to experience love through our human existence? Regarding the people closest to you in your life, it's a soul bond that supersedes space/time and circumstance. When the love is true between two people, it is simply felt no matter what. It's not something that can be "turned on or off". Even if a relationship experience doesn't last for a lifetime, this doesn't make the love connection any less real or substantive. We still love the person and they too love us. While an experience like a relationship may be temporary, the love endures. Most have someone that we love "heart and soul" but will never see again in our life. We don't generally choose who we love and, more to the point, we don't choose who loves us. When it happens, you can choose to let it pass on by, or choose to embrace the experience no matter what happens.

A romantic love experience is often the most powerful, beautiful, yet sometimes difficult and painful. This is especially true if it evolves into a life partner experience. But if the love is true, especially regarding the life partner experience, "love will always find its way" to that highest state of fulfillment! Yes, that is incredibly cliché but it's true. We have free will and we can choose to deny it when it happens. But chances are you would hurt yourself and have a regret if you don't embrace the experience. Love can be the hardest thing to believe in because sometimes it can hurt so bad! Yet, no matter what, the experience of it cannot be denied. When this rare, precious connection happens to you and that precious special someone, let it draw out the best in you and in life and cherish it for all that you truly are, together... love! When we think of this kind of love, we often think of "soul mates" or "twin flames". Basically, these terms are a symbol of the deepest forms of connection of soul love that two people can share. It's not always about romance, but when it is, it can be the most fiery and intense, yet the most gratifying and meaningful of relationships. Love is the ultimate connection because it's like "God's natural vibe". To experience true love is to experience arguably the best part of the divine!

Love is a fundamental function and core quality or constituent of our existence and reality. It exists no matter what and is a key piece of the most fundamental part of our experience intertwined in the fabric of the source consciousness. Yes, it is in the particle reality. These most fundamental quantum particles carry this information as with the information of consciousness. As such, this is inherent in the nature of the field of experiential consciousness, the unified field.

Love or anything associated with love will never impede

on free will. We choose our course of action with respect to choosing to act in love in a given situation. We can choose to ignore it or embrace it. We can let love into all parts of our lives, especially relationships. Or we can choose to make decisions out of selfishness, excess of ego, and fear. The point is, it's our decision.

Money, itself, is not "evil" or unloving. It is about how it is used and the intent behind it. If a person is not grounded in a loving space, an influx of success and money can and often does change them for the worse. Even though wealth makes for certain freedoms, including no longer having to stress over having enough money, many of the world's wealthiest people are unhappy and never feel a sense of fulfillment and completeness. No matter how much is acquired, it's never enough. There always has to be more. However, those with wealth who are in the space of living a loving, abundant life find ways to give back to society. These are people who make a difference. Whether one chooses to live in love or not, that force which is love never changes. It is always there and omnipresent. Love has no bearing on money one way or the other. What matters is the individual intent behind the money or any part of the material experience.

Love means always acting in a capacity that results in what is best for a situation and any people involved, including yourself. Sometimes love asks us to do things that we don't want to do or are difficult. Love may entail making a sacrifice. However, this is something to be careful with. We may find ourselves in a situation where making a sacrifice is an option. If that is the case, never sacrifice for the sake of sacrificing. If you choose to make a sacrifice, make it count. It has to be for the good of someone and/or something. The best thing you can do is follow your heart. Maybe ask yourself, spirit, angels, and/or guidance if it feels right to make a sacrifice? Does if resonate to you? If it feels necessary, then do it. Otherwise, I feel that it is not a loving thing to do to arbitrarily hurt yourself where nothing positive will come out of it. That could arguably be considered a form of martyrdom. Being a martyr especially in getting hurt or damaged is a dark vibrational reality which can perpetuate a negative pattern of thinking you're doing good when you're only hurting yourself and possibly others. Plus, you could be "enabling" a negative pattern in someone else. If this is the case, you may find yourself energetically drained and internally damaged. Either way, this is not an example of sacrificing out of love. The nature of love is to manifest the highest state of fulfillment. Sometimes a sacrifice or the proverbial "step backward to take two steps forward" is best in moving toward fulfillment. The word "fulfillment" can mean a number of things depending on the person(s) and situation(s). That's something we must take time to explore for ourselves.

I contend that the ego is a necessary thing in life as long as life does not become only about ego or about putting the ego first. Ego itself doesn't have to be a bad thing if it's in balance with our deeper areas of consciousness like our soul. The ego is key piece in how we identify with ourselves in the experience of this physical form. As a person in this world, it is at the root of our human personality, value system, and base intent. It's what we show the world and the attributes that come with it. It's also part of our drive, desire, and the will to improve and be the best we can be in whatever our chosen field or the person we choose to be in society. When not in balance, ego can be the thing that "gets in our way" of our personal growth. We've all been around people who were egocentric. Maybe we have experienced being in an egocentric state ourselves when it's all about "me". I feel the ego is most healthy when it's in balance and "listening" to the deeper parts of our consciousness. Such a person tends to know and accept what they are and what they aren't in their life and are comfortable with it. That to me is an example of a healthy and complete ego, or what I term as "total ego". It's a no-nonsense knowing of exactly who you are and who you aren't while being peace with it and grateful for it!

I've learned that ego is necessary to live in society, but the moment a person acts out of self-centeredness and self-importance, it ceases to be love. Excess of ego is when one puts the self ahead of everything else, often to the detriment of the self. Excess of ego does not do what's best for a person or situation, just the self. And that is often questionable. This being stuck in ego or egocentrism depletes love. One must love, take care, and be good to the self. But don't mistake self-importance for being self-love. If one loves and honors the self, there is no room for the delusion of ego excess.

I feel like all these levels of consciousness including ego now have their place in my personal life experience. These different aspects of my being are now essentially working together. My ego has accepted and learned to trust my spiritual guidance. In other words, I'm much more aware of "listening to my intuition or inner voice" or more to the point my "soul self". It's the choice of the ego to trust in that information and what to do with it, if anything. This is that part of us that, in the moment, knows "right from wrong" or more to the point what resonates and what doesn't. In this state, our deeper being or soul being (the part of us that is love) becomes transcendent to our physical level. This reflected in the life decisions I make and the experiences I now attract.

What does it mean to live your life in love? It may at times be the greatest of challenges. One must be at one's strongest, most devoted place within and at their best to walk this path. Doing what's best out of love may yield some excruciatingly difficult life experiences. This is especially true if, like me when I started this part of my journey, you are far from your true self and highest path. It can be years in the making to take steps to "get on that highest path". For me, it started in "baby steps". But like I said, those "baby steps" do start to add up with time.

The experience of love can be deeply damaging to a person. It is not always beauty and softness. Sometimes, these experiences may seem unfair to an individual. They can involve compromising situations. Love certainly isn't weak and it's nobody's "doormat". Yes, love can completely break a person down, leaving them angry, depressed, bitter, and broken. Such a person may never "get over it" and feel completely "broken" inside for their whole life. But regardless of the experience, love can heal any emotional or internal wound and expand the mind, encouraging growth and strength while teaching profound life lessons about connectivity, compassion, and sensitivity. Love is the most powerful force in the universe! It can be just as hurtful as it is healing but for those who have faith in the process, it's all about taking steps towards being at our absolute best!

Love can't help but propel a person to reach to their inner source or the soul, in turn, bringing out the best in them in life. It gives affirmation and clarity in God, the divine, the source, or whatever you choose to call this level of being. Our desires and even our hopes can get in the way of "hearing" what is being conveyed, especially when being caught up in the desire of the carnal side of life. Fear, anger, and anxiety breed self-centeredness. These vibrations can be the most distracting, pulling us away from that loving source within. Being denied things you wish or hope for can leave you feeling forsaken, especially where there is a tragedy and/or trauma. Then there are those times where, "if you ask, you shall receive". However, "be careful what you ask for" and be prepared for the likelihood that what you get may not be what you thought or the way you thought. But if you let it, you understand and embrace that it is what is best for the path.

If living life with love, what you wish and what you get will inherently eventually become one and the same in living in synchronicity and synergy. With love, you can see the path of a situation and bring it to its highest fruition. What you see and "what is" synchronize and become one. Personal exploration through love can completely alter your perception of reality. You will perceive yourself and life much differently. Therefore, your goals and what you want will be different from what they used to be. This has certainly has been the case for me since my experience in opening up to Jesus all those years ago. This culminated with my NDE and the experiences since. Personal exploration can be a very unsettling and frightening thing, depending on the type of person you are and life you may lead when you first make this realization.

So, do you believe in love? Do you believe it is the key to changing your life and even the world? With love, this is not an "I'll try" proposition. To quote Yoda, "Try not. Do or do not. There is no try!" If you believe, you will act and react in kind with love no matter what. Your experience and those connected to the experience will transform.

For a person who lived their life in the mindset that there is only what we perceive with our five senses, a transformation in love may unravel the very fabric of a perception of reality that had been embraced for a lifetime. It could leave a person feeling lost and displaced, especially if said person is in a pattern of focusing on personal gratification from the physical desires and feelings centered around external stimuli like money, materialism, sex, drugs et al. Please understand, I'm not saying these have to be bad things. They don't have to be. But if that is all there is to life for a person, they will likely be feeling empty inside despite the deluge of sensory stimulation. Most people acting in material excess do so because of a feeling of emptiness inside they can't seem to fill. In so doing, they often hurt others.

Finding a loving balance can make all such experiences enjoyable and meaningful. All and any experiences can be part of a loving experience. But like anything in life, it's about balance, perception, and intent. Money, materialism, sex et al can be positive in balance and perspective with a loving heart and intent behind them. Think about music, art, movies, science, education and so on...We live in a capitalized world. If money and materialism are to be part of the experience, like any part of the experience, it's about what's "behind" the use of money and the material and potential outcomes of all of us being affected.

Choosing to reconstruct one's perception of reality and remake the self may be the most difficult choice a person can make. The realization of not knowing who you are can be a frightening and devastating feeling. But it is the first step toward personal discovery, especially the discovery of what true love is. One may have to reinvent themselves and their life inside and out to be able to live a truly loving life. It is generally a process of many years or even a lifetime. This path can completely overwhelm a person as it has me at times. Even with the realization that change is needed, few will endeavor to make that journey in their life given the potential hardships and potential for change along the way. This is an example of finding the strength in love to persevere through any challenges that discovery presents, starting with the love of self!

For as painful and damaging as experiencing love can be, it is the height of vulnerability, compassion, healing, sensitivity, connection, strength, wisdom, and knowledge. Love, especially when shared among people in its pure unselfish form, is beyond comparison with anything we can experience in life. The more you live with love, the more life becomes synergistic and fulfilling in love. The beauty in life becomes more prevalent even amid hardship. But in love, you can take comfort in knowing no matter what you must endure, you can not only persevere but in the long run, completely flourish!

The experience of love, for most, is "bittersweet". It can be emotionally all-consuming, evoking virtually any emotion ranging from destitution to elation. Eternal happiness in life is not realistic, but with love, eternal fulfillment is. Miraculous things can and do happen. God has no meaning and no clear understanding without the experience of love. To know and live love is to know and live in your source soul being or God.

Look at how powerful the impact of love is in any given person's life. Yes, as I've said, love can completely break you down. Far more importantly, love can bring you through the most difficult, traumatic, and tragic of times. No matter how broken down you may seem, love will draw personal strength, strengthen bonds between loved ones, heal the deepest injuries and scars, and at the same time bring about truly meaningful and transformational experiences in life. Love can clear away unhealthy patterns by healing and releasing one's past. Love impacts to the core of one's personal beliefs and makes way for new opportunities and ways of thinking and being.

Consider the difference a person can make for those around them when they act in love for the best interest of everyone and everything. Love can bring out the best in a person and in a life. Imagine if we could spent our childhood in a world where the standard practice was the commitment to love for all. So many of the issues and divisions in the world like war, killing, stealing, racial and religious prejudices, greed, and all that is accepted as commonplace between different people around the world simply wouldn't exist. It would be unfathomable to consider doing anything hurtful to one another because in such a world, we feel together. The need for power, greed, violence, hatred would become obsolete. Through love, we could be all be living the life of our dreams in the world of our dreams.

Here's an exercise... Can you look in the mirror looking deeply and longingly into your own eyes and say with heartfelt passion, "I love you"? If the answer is "no", perhaps search your heart for that all-important self-compassion. How can we truly love anyone or anything if we don't truly love ourselves? It starts with you... and me!

SPIRIT

Spirit is that which gives rise to life. It is the fundamental quality that is life itself. It's what drives the will "to be". This includes everything that is life, including the source consciousness itself. Spirit is the pure essence of life. Mind you, this doesn't specifically pertain to organic life. To be considered organic, certain scientific standards apply as per science. But in the case of spirit, the reference to life goes well beyond the organic. For everything from a fundamental particle to a prospective multiverse, I'm suggesting that it's all alive as per the divine source consciousness itself. An electron, atom, cell, planet, star, galaxy, and universe are all experiencing some form of life process and experience.

Spirit and soul are directly synonymous. Both represent the source and the purest essence of life and the life experience. However, while spirit is the underlying driving force that is life, the soul is the sentient perceptual experience of life or lives as is often perceived with respect to beliefs about karma.

Spirit is also referred to as Chi, prana, Shakti, mana, among others. It is the life essence of being. It is all that gives rise to existence. It is through spirit that love and mind are drawn out or are "born" from the field of consciousness. In a way, spirit is the birth of the experience as the birth of life and even the birth of pure being itself (as an initial "spark" of life, as it is forever and omni-present). Spirit is that which is the source of life and that which is alive. All organic beings and non-organic or inanimate objects have spirit. In short, it's all alive. Even that which is not organic is nonetheless alive. It's all part of the divine experiential embodiment. Because the divine is the source and essence of spirit, it is alive. All that is a part of this singular divine embodiment is alive. All that is a part of our lives including everything that's alive and organic as well as objects or things like cars, houses, computers or even a rock, a piece of steel, or fossil fuels like oil and gas are a part of or have spirit. In this respect, they are all alive. All that which comes from the life source, even that which is non-organic, has spirit. That is because it all stems from the mind of the same single divine source, being life force or spirit – i.e. the will that sprang creation into motion in the first place. It's the will to be, even for the divine!

Nature and the elements all have a life force. I now understand the anthropomorphism and the deification of nature that has been a common practice throughout history and prehistory. There are and have been many gods of nature or representing aspects of nature. Native Americans, many other native peoples in different forms of Shamanism around the world, and those that practice Druidism, Wicca, and other nature-based practices, recognize a life essence to the different areas and aspects of nature and in nature itself. Even a gust of wind has a life force. A cool soft evening breeze blowing gently for a just a moment or lukewarm midsummer shower has a life force of its own. Each begins, grows and peaks, subsides, and perishes. But a simple gust of wind is just one part of the complex pattern of currents of so many other parts working together in synergy. Some of the bigger more powerful things in nature were and are recognized as gods. These "gods" are nature and are in nature. The gods are found in the weather, especially where certain conditions at a certain time of year are good for growing food. If during a growing season, the weather conditions do not provide enough water for crops, people may starve. People who practice nature-based beliefs believe that nature and the Earth are alive, with everything working in synergy. Clearly, the Earth is very much having her own life experience. The Earth has her own life force or spirit. The Earth has an incredibly complex, multi-layered energy dynamic. We can pick any one thing in any time period of the Earth and have a lifetime of study. Never mind getting into the dynamics of the Earth's geological and evolutionary processes. What a truly spectacular experience it's been!

As this planet Earth is alive, I relate to the reference "Mother Earth". The Earth is our bearer of life. A plethora of life has sprang up on or near her surface, possibly beginning with mound-forming bacteria called stromatolites about 3.8 billion years ago. Some scientists have suggested that life could have started as early as a couple hundred million years after the Earth's birth about 4.5 billion years ago. All her forces are part of a complex collection of forces and that life essence or spirit giving us our organic life experience. The life of Mother Earth propagates life evolving from a single celled form of bacteria to the billions of the complex life forms that have evolved since. While the Earth has endured major catastrophes, the Earth's conditions have been favorable throughout most of this time for the evolution of life.

Spirit is still that force of "chi" or "prana" that is the "heart" that gives this "spark" to ignite life on Earth from an inorganic chemical soup, even as a completely rudimentary form of experiential consciousness and sentience. Life on Earth has endured massive bombardments and been incased in a planet wide ball of ice. Tectonic forces have created super-volcanos and massive earth-quakes. Life has been on the brink of total extinction possibly five times. Some scientists believe we are on the verge of a sixth. However, life, in one form or another, has persevered and had the benefit of time to evolve between these catastrophes.

Then there are forces like the weather. This includes the wind, rain, thunder, lightning, snow, hail, tidal waves and clouds, not to mention massive storms like hurricanes, cyclones, blizzards, and typhoons. The weather can cause tremendous heatwaves and droughts. All these weather forces work together in a global synergy, causing a variety of weather patterns all over the planet. Separately, each of these weather patterns or storms has a veritable sense of life, consciousness, and experience. Each of the pieces of the overall system works within the lifecycle of larger systems and one singular worldwide system. There is the point of generation or birth, growth and peak, and eventually subsiding and death. Smaller systems give way to new weather patterns and systems, all as part of the total life cycle. It's a life cycle that extends out to the totality of the Earth. On this scale, it's one weather system, one Earth, with a great many detailed and intricate characteristics and actions happening within the planet's atmosphere.

The planet has tectonic forces at work, all part of spirit with their own life essence. Giant plates move over the planetary crust, causing tremors and earthquakes, tsunamis, volcanism, geysers, and sinkholes. All of these have served both to nurture and support the growth of life and as cause of extinctions. Ask any geologist: they will tell you a long, complex, and integrated tectonic story instrumental to the evolution of life and the Earth herself. Each tectonic process, earthquake, volcano, tsunami, and so on has a life force, impact on the environment, and experience of its own as parts of the life force of the Earth.

All such forces of nature and its basic constituents, traditionally referred to as the elements of earth, air, water, and fire, may include the astral and the ether depending on the spiritual practice and philosophy. I consider the term "astral" as simply a name or reference to space and the stars in the sky before we knew a bit about what is really out there. But even still the term "astral" can also be a reflection of what we still don't know about these vast expanses of infinite energy. But I refer to that level of existence as the astral or astral energy. To me, the ether is the equivalent to the quantum levels. It's the space in between the nucleus and the electrons of an atom and between atoms also with infinite energy in the subatomic expanses. Atoms after all barely have or are discernible matter. The atom is primarily space. An atom seems to be an empty subatomic vacuum, but in effect, it's pure vibrational energy, especially with electrons popping in and out of existence in a patternistic fashion around the atomic nucleus. A particle can change from a photon to an electron to a proton to a neutrino based on vibration. As the vibration changes so does the particle. Oh, but wait - the nucleus pops in and out of existence too as does the entire atom. No matter, this generates the vibration that reflects in the existence of these particles and atoms. These atoms vibrate to form bonds with other atoms and become molecules. The ether is a base field of energy that is a sort of harmonic filter turning these atomic vibrations into discernable (to us) matter at the atomic and molecular level. This is an intangible type of energy or force that makes the atom and its particles vibrate in harmony with one another and come together to create atomic structures. Underlying atoms, the "building blocks" of matter and our reality, is the spirit that is the essence of the will to give rise to these atomic structures. This in turn gives rise to the molecules and matter. Whether you prefer the more spiritual explanation or maybe something more quantum or scientific, spirit, a part of the source consciousness, is that wish, that desire, that "will to be" as a particle or as God.

Spiritually, this ether reflects the deeper levels of consciousness and being between the unified field/source of consciousness and the formation of matter with which we begin to identify at the atomic and molecular level. All of this is experienced through the source being within. Space/time is a reality here yet a blended one in which lifetimes and the ages of time are mere thoughts. Much of our life is based in our imagination, dreams, intuition, feelings, empathy, and that which is considered psychic ability. In other words, that which is experienced beyond the five senses. These bodies and our senses are "tools and mechanisms" with which to experience in the world in these bodies living our lives. Spirit is what makes it all live!

All things bear a life force. Spirit is at the basis of everything alive including these seemingly hard to grasp areas of existence and being like the ether and astral or the quanta or space. Everything is alive even that which isn't organic. It is all based in and bears spirit.

Now this may be hard to fathom and seem counter intuitive, but even while inanimate objects have spirit, the experience is clearly much different. Inanimate objects experience on a completely rudimentary level. They don't have the means to have an experience like a being of any level of sentience. An inanimate or inorganic object has nothing approaching a brain or even any organic body with a semblance of a central nervous system or nucleus as is found in single celled organisms. Even these single celled organisms have the means to have or express some form of an experience with which we can identify on some level, however rudimentary. For inanimate objects, there is consciousness but there is no sentience with which to express or identify with the experience.

But these inanimate objects are still an extension of that core source consciousness. This core source is alive, so that which comes from it too is alive. This includes inorganic matter having an inorganic existence and experience. Things like a chair, car, house, or anything along those lines run their course in terms of its creation, span of existence, and demise. In other words, such things too, in a manner of speaking, are born, are built or evolve to completion or maturity, have a "prime", get old, deteriorate, and eventually perish or die. Such "things" may not have the ability to understand an experience and to express it the way we do, but they are nonetheless a form of experience with their own life energy, life span, and impact to existence. Their existence and invariably what happens to them is information that is part of the fabric of the source conscious field or the unified field. This can be understood as the conservation of information, the Akashic Records, or simply a thought field consisting of every possible piece of information including the experience of a seemingly innocuous inanimate object.

Inanimate objects are still part of the core essence of consciousness and part of all that is connected. Therefore, they are part of God experiencing God's self, just not in a way with which we are able to identify or relate. As mentioned, God is the experience of everything. That includes these inanimate objects. Therefore, all things have spirit born out of the same will to be as spirit itself.

Each experience, situation, or being, no matter how great or small, has the spirit energy. Spirit is the life force for all things. Spirit literally brings everything to life. Such things, whether organic in nature or not, take on a life energy and experience of their own. Reality itself has a basis in spirit and consciousness. Reality is the life force. It's all spirit.

Spirit is that which perpetuates the life of the infinity of the divine experience. The one soul of God, that which is our soul, is life or spirit in its purist form. Spirit is that life essence at source. Because spirit is alive at the source and because this source infuses life into everything that is, it's is all very much alive. It all has a life vibration unto itself that each of us can feel. It's always moving, growing, changing, starting, ending, and evolving into many possibilities. To coin Dr. Frankenstein, "It's alive!"

MIND

Mind is the thought and imagination of this divine being. To coin a phrase from theoretical physicist Jonathan Hagelin, "we live in a thought universe". Think of reality of as a visualization of the divine mind. All of reality as we know it and the entirety of the universe is a reflection of this mind. It is this source mind that perpetuates intent of thoughts of love and spirit, drawing it out of consciousness in its perception of the experience.

The brain is a transceiver of mind, essentially interpreting the experience in a way that makes sense to the brain. This creates a perception of reality and experience for each one of us. The brain oscillates mind both internally and externally on every level. It receives information from the unified level of reality at the source of consciousness. It also receives information from the environment stemming from the body and physical senses. Even this can be quite vast, as far as the eye can see, even out to the cosmos while staring into a star-filled night sky. The brain responds to both internal and external stimuli and responds in kind, performing functions as a mechanism while generating a perception of an experience of reality for each us in our respective brains as individual people.

The brain in fact has access to all the information of existence and the creation of the universe given its own inherent connection to the quantum reality. So too, does our heart (some suggest this is largely area for experiencing feelings and intuition) and the rest of our entire body, but the brain is a key component to our subjective interpretation of reality. This is in addition to the ways our very atoms are connected to the makeup of the Earth, past exploded stars, and our universal origins as well as our inherent connection with the unified field, the source of consciousness. The information of "the all" is contained within and all around us.

While there is an aspect of the consciousness of God

that exists moving through space/time as we do, generating the creation experiencing as we do moment by moment, the true source of God comes from a singularity where "the all" of everything is one all-encompassing wave of probabilities and possibilities in all of space/time all at once. To perceive God from the perspective of a mind that exists in all space/time, including all possibility and probability, and in all dimensions, is to perceive the mind of the divine as a wavelike field of energy like the unified field. This is a mind that contains the thought information of all the infinite possibilities of existence and experience. It is just a matter of perspective to see it as a singular whole or as a single isolated moment of space/time on an "arrow of time". Perspective may also dictate how complex and vast or how simplistic and minute the singularity of source consciousness may appear to one's mind. This includes and encompasses ideals of parallel universes and multiple worlds theories, suggesting the mind of God consists of many such singularities with endless possibilities that ultimately coalesce into a single mind and consciousness at the source.

Looking at the mind of the consciousness of God from a perspective that encompasses "the all" would mean, to God, this is a completed picture that is yet viewed as a single moment unto itself. Consider the aspect where the evolution of God transpires from the perspective of moment-by-moment linear existence. Like us, God exists or at least appears to exist from our human viewpoint growing and evolving moment by moment in this state of being in space/time and universal law, including the many aspects of these laws we don't yet understand. Of course, while our understanding of universal law has grown immensely, we still know only a small bit of these laws. The magic of yesterday is the science of today and the magic of today will be the science of tomorrow.

For God to pick a point in time to experience from "the all" perspective would be like recalling a memory, but it's really not. God is always "in the moment" yet still is "the all". Consider a solitary moment as such: a single embodiment of the infinite embodiments all at once. This moment comes from the whole singular realm of probability and possibility. This realm, the "God perspective", has the ability to "zero in" or "collapse" on a moment from the infinite "wave" of possibilities, creating certainty out of uncertainty as the "Ultimate Observer" to the infinite experiences. Each moment stems from and collapses from that which is "the all". This includes something as small and finite as an observed particle in space/time to the whole of a multiverse and any point in between, regardless of the scale of space/time or perception of the reality.

This is the soul of God and the source of creation. The entirety of creation is all a reflection of this source of consciousness experiencing itself through this infinite source of existence. This is the source level of reality where everything that is reality exists in a state of perpetual superposition, meaning the all of everything existing at once. It's like the wave versus the particle. The aspect of the totality of reality existing in this state of superposition is the wave. This is where everything that is the total reality, existence, and experience, is in a state of pure probability and possibility. When you "collapse" to a moment of reality on the "arrow of time", this is like collapsing the wave, such as a light wave, when seeking to observe or measure a photon. When you collapse the wave, all you appear to have is the photon. This is just like a moment of space/time for us. This single source consciousness experiences in the moment as it is the experience of "the all". This is the source of all that was, is, and ever will be; consciousness, divinity, and the unified field!

However, given that from our human perspective, this divine conscious experience from the fundamental particle all the way out to a singular super macrocosmic existence exists in linear space/time as we do (how that works is another story), the universal consciousness is constantly splitting itself off to infinite realities from infinite possibilities, but as parts of the ultimate whole mind experiencing an ultimate grand experience. Therefore, this makes mind "all knowing" because the information of every possibility and probability is all already contained therein that ultimate mind. Yet these experiences still have to be carried out and created to be actual experiences in the overall experience.

We are part of that single divine experience. Think about the perceptions of space/time from the stand point of an electron, atom, cell, human, solar system, galaxy or the whole Universe. The closer you get to the perception of the universal whole, the slower the perception of space/time, to that point where past, present, and future are all one in the same. What could that possibly mean to a multiuniversal existence? Travel at the "speed of thought".

All the qualities, carnal and spiritual, existing in the world as we know it, wouldn't exist if they weren't already inherent in that core source consciousness. This includes absolutely everything in our lives, right down to our individual thoughts, ideas, beliefs, philosophies, desires, dreams, and feelings, especially love, spirit, and mind. We are all, on a fundamental level, like small independent pieces of consciousness in the ultimate consciousness of God perceived as a part of the source of mind.

We are perceived by God in the moment of the experience just as we may perceive God. This source consciousness sees, feels, and experiences through each of us as we may see, feel, and experience through source consciousness. This universal entity is alive and conscious through God at the source just as we ourselves are alive and conscious. The true essence of the source of God is pure consciousness and pure being in love, spirit, and mind. This essence is pure eternal consciousness and being, generating in all of the embodied multi-universal creation, whatever that may truly entail, including a thought. This entire reality consisting of the whole multiverse is reflection of this vast divine mind. Therefore, it is all God - conscious and sentient!

Now for the human brain to interpret the information from the mind of God or that point of pure consciousness is certainly possible. That's part of the point of the Gravity series. However, this can be likened to having an elite level high wattage professional amplifier hooked up to a pair of cheap 30-year-old generic brand low wattage speakers. If you hook up the amplifier to a quality iPod or CD player and play your favorite song, it would work. You would be able to hear your song; however, it would only be as loud and sound as good as those speakers would allow. The speakers' limits on the performance of power and the resolution compared to the amplifier would be quickly maximized. Those speakers at their best would only reflect a small fraction of that amplifier's capacity to perform. Basically, this analogy means that while we have the information of the universe and existence available to us, it must process through our human brains in this given point in our experience and in time. The human brain is still the most sophisticated mechanism known to humanity and while we still don't know its true potential, it is still only able to process and comprehend a small portion of this immense breadth of information from a divine or universal "download". Of course that is part of our evolution and growth both physically, consciously, and spiritually. The more we explore and experience, the more we can grow, learn, and understand.

Our human mind and the divine mind are one and the same. That's something we see as we awaken to the divine mind from this slumber that has become many of our lives. The source of all knowledge, experience, thought and imagination are connected. Every experiential thought is part of everything and part of all of us!

CONSCIOUSNESS

Consciousness is at the core source of all that is. It is in everything and is everywhere. At its root, it is the field of every possible experience and subjective interpretation therein. The source observer and experiencer is intricately intertwined in its divine perspective through the conscious experience of every one of us. This whole experiential process is still the experience of our consciousness or soul and consequently the experience of that divine source. It is that which harbors, encompasses, and permeates everything, fusing love, spirit, and mind as the true source of all existence and the true "heart" of God. When attempting to explain and define the core level of reality (regardless of what you choose to call it), the spiritual explanation referring to a "field consciousness" is the same as the scientific or quantum expression of the unified field.

This source level of reality or "field of consciousness" is the ultimate state of quantum superposition. Superposition basically says that particles can exist in multiple places at the same time. The unified level of reality is every possible reality existing in multiple places at once. It's a field of conscious possibilities. This is the space where everything imaginable originates and is all one. There is no differentiation from anything like light/dark, male/female, positive/negative, or even good/evil. The fundamental basis of existence - all of creation, matter, and all that is existence in any reality or universe that is contained in and emerging from this consciousness or unified field - is a pure field, free of intention. It just is. This ultimate consciousness is the ultimate conscious experience as every possible reality.

Consciousness is basically referring to a sense of personal being and deeper aspects like connectivity, the divine, empathy, intuition et al in the experience. This is in contrast to sentience, which is more directly about an awareness of self in the experience, whether as a person or a soul being. Not everything that bears consciousness has sentience. An experience can involve some form of conscious experience without any sentience, like a chair. However, sentience cannot exist without consciousness. This is why consciousness, not sentience, is still "the floor". But then there more questions. Are chimpanzees, dolphins, dogs, cats or any other animals sentient or for that matter do they have any form of consciousness? What about plants and trees or algae, or a single celled bacterium? How about the possibility for consciousness of the Earth, the Sun, the stars and galaxy? And how about the consciousness of a table, a car or any number of inorganic inanimate objects? Simply put, it's all consciousness but not all sentience or varying levels of sentience. Yet the core source is not only purely conscious of all but also purely sentient per the experience of all. All of existence is the result of thoughts of the source mind, being brought to life through spirit, and "lifted up" to the ultimate state of fulfillment through love in a state of pure being.

Personally, I feel an energy emanating from all such things from organic life to inanimate objects that feel alive. When I drive my car I do have a certain connection and intuition about the car itself. There is also a feeling of mind and being with these objects because of the source. Each different landscape, each human made structure, and each celestial body has its own energy signature and life force. It's all emanating from the source consciousness.

Touching upon intuition and empathy, many of us get feelings about people or about being in certain surroundings. It could be a location, area, building, or a room. Sometimes it feels welcoming or loving; sometimes it feels somehow unsettling or downright negative and repulsive. We may feel like we want to leave a certain place. Some places or locations just feel miserable or simply "dark". This is all part of that life force or spirit energy emanating from the source level. While that which science considers to be nature is certainly alive, that body of water we call a lake or a sea or that giant piece of protruding rock we call a mountain has consciousness as per its experience. Again, it certainly isn't anything we can currently identify with, but that essence of consciousness is there at the source of its existence as the most fundamental part of its experience.

Life forces take on many forms, especially regarding consciousness. Varying groups of people have a form of collective consciousness. It can be a family, a couple, or a pair of friends co-creating a singular conscious experience. We all most likely know pairs of people who, when together, create a certain vibe and chemistry that can be empathically felt. All relationships are a form of consciousness unto themselves. The chemistry between all people on any level of interaction has that collective singular vibe or energy experiencing as a form of consciousness unto itself.

Think about larger groups of say 10 people, 1000 people, or millions if not billions of people. Think of the feel of going to a Rock concert versus a big Electronic music festival versus a symphony concert. All may be amazing in their own right, but each has its own feel, vibe, or energy. Each is its own form of conscious life experience. How about a football game or any sports competition? Each team and each game has a certain feel or energy. Each game in each sport has its own energy signature. Ask any athlete or fan - the regular season of a sport feels totally different than the energy of the playoffs or the championship! Each has its own feel, especially taking this from the vantage point of the participant versus the spectator.

Think about the feel of being in a city like Denver, then going to New York. From there, go to Tokyo. Each city has its own feeling to it. Each city is unique with its own vibrational signature or life force. Even globally there is a feel to the world.

Think about or imagine the feel of the world during World War 2 or the feel of the world during the height of the Roman Empire versus now. There is collective life force to everything on every level and scope of reality. These energies, like with everything, have a beginning or a birth, they grow and peak, and then they begin to subside and perish. Every perspective and perception of every level of consciousness has a life experience of its own. It is all consciousness.

Consciousness at the source generates and creates matter, not the other way around. As described, it's all conscious and alive. Matter, unto itself, does not create and generate consciousness. It is part of the conscious experience. Consciousness is necessary with respect to having any form of experience, regardless of the level of sentience.

Love, spirit, and mind at the source are all the beauties of life where you find and draw on the true substance and permanence of this source consciousness. Love, spirit, and mind bring consciousness to life and to the experience of all. This collective experience connecting together each experience, person, soul expanding into divine consciousness is the ultimate experience, whether incarnated as a human or existing as a soul being moving through different incarnations!

How do you measure love, spirit, or mind? How do you measure a thought, especially with respect to where it truly originates in mind and is processed through the brain? Where there is the beauty and purity of love, the innocence of life from spirit, and the purity of thought and imagination from mind, there is the true source of divine consciousness or God. Each is synonymous with the other. The experience of consciousness can take many paths and be experienced many ways. Sometimes it's incredibly difficult, but it is the ultimate experience and is the journey home.

Each facet described here – love, mind, spirit, and consciousness – is in a sense a different way to explain or experience different aspects of these same basic things at the same core source level of being. Quite simply, love is spirit, mind, and consciousness; spirit is love, mind and consciousness; mind is love, spirit, and consciousness; and consciousness is love, spirit, and mind. They are different aspects of the experience while being the source of the experience itself.

6

The Return of Dreams

In the time since my NDE, I've come to realize that this feeling that I have "awakened" wasn't just about the NDE but rather began with the NDE. However, I can trace it further back. Naturally, this began with my birth into this life. I can see the connectivity and synchronicity of all the moments and events of my life. As far as making the conscious choice to "open the doors" to a higher understanding and discovering my highest path, I feel it was when I prayed to Jesus for the first time just before my mother died, especially when I said, "I want to know what you know and see what you see." I couldn't understand why, despite how promising my future in business and finance looked, I felt so empty. I needed answers! That is when the stripping away of everything I thought I was supposed to be began. But my personal turning point and subsequent transformation is unequivocally my NDE. Immediately after it happened and shortly thereafter, I was already feeling that something significant was within me and around me. I could feel the percolations of thoughts I had either forgotten about or never knew I had. I slept a lot, especially in that first year after the fall. During that time, I began experiencing some of the most vivid and lucid dreams I had experienced since being a child. I was finding that these dreams were direct reflections of my waking reality. The dreams, like the moment of being near-death I discussed earlier, became a very lucid thought process. However, it was just the beginning in transitioning dreams from one reality to another, from the sleeping reality to the waking dream.

It has since been a deep process that at many points along the way could have taken me into a potential for further distraction. I could have returned to rerunning old patterns or just simply settling for an experience that more than likely may not benefit and support my highest life path. My imagination has come alive with dreams in a way new to me, especially all of these epiphanies, but these dreams are ancient in that they have always been with me, as with us all. The dreaming – whether sleeping or waking – has become something much different than when I was a child. It is taking me into realms of thought where I feel universally and consciously expanded. I've never felt so free! This awakening has meant a great deal of healing and releasing the negative or that which does not support my path in this moment and embracing the wonders, beauty, and love of life!

An interesting thing happened that, for me, brings the dreams full circle. While I have evolved in my dreams and visions and, as such, my thought processes, I have somehow rediscovered the "child within", very nearly a…"Return to Innocence". Yes, that is a reference to the Enigma song of the same name. I sometimes tear up when I hear it because the words and the music simply resonate. No, I will never proclaim to be innocent. I am most certainly anything but, although something innocent and childlike has awoken inside me. I haven't felt this since long before my mother died. Now with all my new-found visions, I am once again dreaming as I did when I was a child and young man. That, I have discovered, is the key to the manifestation of the life that is morphing before me now.

Not to take away from the powerful experiences of my

past, but I seem to have a certain internal malleability with growing into this new path. Not unlike when we are toddlers, I feel this openness and flexibility to a potentially dramatic growing and learning process as the person I am on this ever-evolving path. There have been some profound moments that have been integral in the sculpting and creation of the person I am now and the person I'm still yet becoming. In some ways, these have been some of my most revealing and defining of my life experiences. After all, I can feel that this is a time to "build my personal foundation upon which to build my future" and prepare myself in being at my best for wonders to come! I feel I have grown more in the years since my NDE than at any other point in my life. This has all been crucial to my preparation for not just this next phase of my life but for the rest of my life, which most certainly includes the writing and releasing of this book. For me, after many years of working on it, it's a big step forward!

A rather challenging dynamic presented itself as I was just months removed from getting out of the hospital. One of my long-time dear friends discovered she had cancer. It was "supposed" to be curable. "Supposedly" the doctors found it early. As far as cancer treatment goes, it was "supposed" to be relatively routine. After a couple years-long battle with cancer, she died. I think she was 31 years old.

I'd known my friend, Christi, for some 12 or so years. She was beautiful and vibrant! Just her walking into a room made the place brighter. She always had a smile on her face and a hug for everyone. Not only was she "model" beautiful, but she had an authentic beauty about her as the person she was. That was reflected in how many people absolutely loved her including me! Her passing hit a lot of people really hard! The general feeling was that world needs people like Christi and that she shouldn't have been taken so young.

As an example of the friend she was to me, she helped

put together one of the benefit events friends held for me after I got out of the hospital. She was involved in putting it together with longtime close friend (and brother) and former business partner Kaya, aka, DJ Kaya. They really went "all out"! Plus, this event marked the first time I felt well enough to get out for a few hours. Christi and Kaya worked hard to make the event happen! There were lots of amazing DJs and go-go dancers! Plus, there were lots of friends who came. Kaya made some custom video which was super cool! I even DJ'd a set. I wasn't moving too fast and still using a cane to assist in walking. One may have thought I was elderly at 44. But I did play a short set. I really needed that at that time! Christi was just her beautiful, amazing self! Kaya too was amazing! I'm grateful that she was a part of making that experience happen. It was such a total blast! To which I was and still am super grateful!

At her funeral there must have been a couple hundred people. It was amazing! I saw lots of people I hadn't seen for a while. I appreciated that! Yet, there some emotionally difficult moments. I had a conversation with a girl who was one of Christi's longtime close friends. She was understandably devastated! I know this was more the result of the grieving for her dear friend, but we had, what was for me, a rather difficult conversation. This has no bearing on the fact she is a sweet person and would never wish me or certainly anyone harm but there were the suggestion of why someone so light and beautiful like Christi would die from something many thought she would survive and I survived something I probably shouldn't have. Speaking with Christi's boyfriend was also a difficult part of the funeral. I fully understand that he too was also absolutely devastated. I'm not going to presume to speak for him, but I felt a lot of anger from him towards me. Yes, no doubt he was in the middle of the hardest, most painful time in his life! The love of his life had just died! He made several comments about how special she was. But it wasn't in a friendly sense of reminiscing.

There was anger in his voice. He reminded me I was lucky to have Christi as a friend. Naturally, I completely agreed! But I can't help wondering that he too felt a certain resentment, in the moment, towards me, not unlike Christi's friend. Whether that was the case or not, like Christi, he is an awesome person and had been a good friend over the years! While it hurt at the time, I do understand and feel nothing but love for Christi's boyfriend and friend! I've not seen them since but I would hope if we do see each other, it can be met with hugs!

After Christi's death, I began to struggle with why someone like Christi, who when originally diagnosed with cancer was told she was going be ok, would die, and someone like me, while a nice person, but still quite dark and angry inside, would survive. Even if those difficult conversations at the funeral hadn't happened, I would still have struggled with this. I believe the term is "survivor's remorse". I had lots of great friends who stepped up on my behalf in many wonderful ways while I was in the hospital and the time after going through my surgeries. One of the things that helped motivate me was realizing how many awesome friends I had, and still have! For that I will always be immensely grateful! Christi had a love from the community that was, simply put, special! It was just on "another level". She touched many people in precious ways. I began to think, why wasn't that me instead of her? She was a much brighter light than I was, still subdued in my darkness. I would have gladly switched places with her!! Of course, that's not the way life and the experience work. Despite the difficulty and seeming unfairness of Christi's death, I realized and (had to) accept all is as it should be.

What was or am I going to do about this moving forward? While she was a dear wonderful friend, within my life experiences, she may not have had the same influence as my mother, Micki, or my Uncle Bill. However, she was a positive part of my life for many years and was a truly rare, special person! She has become part of my motivation and inspiration to be the best person that I can be in leaving a positive mark on the world by the time I do die. All the fun memories, all of the laughs, the awesome hugs, and her bright beautiful smile and spirit will always be an important part of me and my experience especially now and moving forward!

Sometimes you just never know what or whom will touch you your heart. When your heart is open, you never know with whom you might connect. One of my best friends is Minnie Collins! Minnie is a mother, grandmother, great-grandmother, great-great-grandmother, and a best friend to my mother... She is a beautiful woman from Kansas who epitomizes class and manners. She is among the most precious and authentic of people I have ever met in my life! I love this woman! The entire Collins family is huge, spread out all over the country. I think it is safe to say she is the family elder or matriarch. Minnie is a big part of what makes that family so strong! I'm sure like any big family it has its dramas and disagreements. But no matter what, every member of this family wouldn't hesitate to "step up" for any other member of the family. "The force is strong with this family" (if I may borrow a "Star Wars" quote)! Her son, Elliot, had been dating my mother for about two years up until my mother passed. Elliot, who is now deceased, was a wonderful boyfriend to my mother and a great friend to me! His sister, Minnie's daughter, Burdell, was also one of my mother's closest friends! Burdell, like my mother and her mother, was/is the epitome of a strong beautiful woman! I met Minnie, Elliot, and Burdell in 1986. Somehow Minnie has always managed to stay in touch. Because of my friendship with Minnie and our connection, I am blessed to know this amazing family for so many years!

Sometimes a group of people that you may not expect can touch you. Minnie is a long-time member of Prince of Peace Church (her husband, Reverend Theodore Collins, spent his life as a pastor until his passing and was a truly beautiful soul). I spent some time attending this church shortly after my NDE. Prince of Peace is a Pentecostal church. Pentecostals, not unlike Southern Baptists and other more fundamentalist Christian practices, are often seen as fanatical and judgmental. I spent some time attending Prince of Peace initially to spend some time with Minnie. I also thought it was a great opportunity to learn about Pentecostalism, this perception of the divine, and the energy of this group of people. I anticipated that it would be an illuminating experience, but I must say was pleasantly surprised by just how deeply illuminating and endearing it was and how much I came to love this church and its people!

I found Prince of Peace to be filled with people with a true passion for Jesus Christ. They truly do believe with a deep love in each and every one of their hearts! Given my NDE and the insights it has allotted me, there are obviously going to be some distinct differences in how we perceive the divine or God. But regardless, their love and devotion is as real or true as with any group I've spent time with. I have a different perception about God, consciousness, spirituality, et al. But our love, our passion, are equally as real and true! I can't express just how much love I have felt from all the church's members towards me and to each other. This group is passionate about everything especially with respect to their service. The music is pure energy! The music was my favorite part! As someone who spent years in the music business including artist development, I was constantly impressed with the level of talent considering the church is fairly small. When the music started, everybody got into it! Everyone would start singing along and dancing, sometimes all over the room. Yes, of course, I was singing and dancing too. I often left a service on an awesome "natural life high", a feeling I seldom have had when leaving most church services. What can I say, I love Prince of Peace Church! They are such a genuine, loving group of people who are doing their best to honor their path and experience! While our perceptions may be different, it's all still lived in love!

Pastor Brent and First Lady Carla Coburn are the church leaders. Both are wonderfully real and loving people! They really do live and breathe the love they preach. I had the pleasure of having dinner with these genuine and loving people one evening. We had some deep, intelligent conversations. I shared the story of my NDE and some of my epiphanies with them. Instead of "shooting down" my thoughts or telling me "it's the devil" (which I have heard), they basically said, "You're one deep dude." I really enjoyed the conversations and our time together! I have an immense respect and love for the both of them! When Pastor Brent preaches, I know he preaches from the heart!

Something rather serendipitous happened that also put into perspective the importance of these past, often difficult to take, experiences and their meaning in my life now. I was hanging out in one of my favorite coffee shops/book stores with some friends having a spiritual conversation. We were mainly discussing love. A young man in his early to mid-20's was eavesdropping from a nearby table. Having spent time on the streets and having friends whom may be considered "street", it was clear to me this guy was right off the "street" himself. He had a hard energy, at least on the surface in the way he moved and talked. He also had what I am pretty sure were prison tattoos. No, I have not been to prison, but I know what tattoos done in prison look like. Getting tattooed in prison is a different process than in a professional shop so they have a different look. If he did get those tats in prison, he may have been quite young, possibly 18 or maybe as young as 17 going in. Anyway, he was sitting with a friend of his who had a similar way about him. This guy moves his chair over close to mine and sits down facing me. He says something like, "Man, you don't know s**t! You talkin' all this love bulls**t!? You ever see life on the streets? You ever see a real ghetto? Do you even watch the news? You wouldn't last day on the streets. The streets would chew you up and spit you out. You soft!" He was genuinely serious, almost like he was almost mad at me for talking as I was.

Obviously, I had "pushed a button" in something I said. So, I took my glasses off, set them on the table, turned my chair to look him directly in the eyes, and said, "Don't think you have me figured out, you have no idea. But I'm about to tell you...". I proceeded to share a couple things from my past he would relate to. I then told him about my NDE and what happened coma, broken bones, et al. I asked him how he would have handled something like that if it happened to him. I said, "So, how strong are you really?" He had a bit of a surprised smile on his face and had a moment of hesitation. The young man shook his head and said, "Can I get in on this?" He did as did his friend. He proved to be most intelligent and insightful and a welcome participant in the discussions. Even his friend, while mostly quiet, chimed in a few times. That was awesome!! I can't say what he did with that experience with respect to his life after-the-fact. But perhaps, at the least, it was "some positive seeds planted that could take root" at any time, whether since then or even years from now. Suddenly, this "terrible" past of mine had some positive meaning! My past really has set me free. Now, I really could let it all go. Those old burdens have finally been lifted. I never would have imagined this, but it's amazing what can happen when you look at and approach life through loving eyes. Even the dark can become light! After all, as per the First Law of Thermodynamics, "...energy is always changing states". Yes, these concepts of "light and dark" too have their energetic vibrational frequencies.

I had profound soul experience with a special woman. It was with a woman who was beautiful, intelligent, talented, and incredibly deep! She's the type of person who not only can do what she sets her mind to but will likely excel at it. We shared an experience of love with deep karmic connections. Our experience was the epitome of bittersweet. On the one-hand, it was most difficult and painful. After we said our "good-byes", I felt drained and exhausted. I imagine she may have too. This experience was hard on the both of us. On the other hand, the experience had elements of truly intimate, tender, and beautiful moments! It was the sharing of a connection unlike any other I had known. As much as I have loved the women from my past, this was the only time there was even a consideration of the possibility that I had found the love and connection of the woman with whom I would grow old. There were times it felt that way. This is what I dreamed about as a child.

Like many of life's deepest experiences, this being no exception, there were many things that came "bubbling to the surface" from it, both light and dark. Starting a little closer to the experience itself, I had an opportunity to hone my intuition, or psychic ability as she would prefer to describe it, with a variety of psychic classes. She is a talented psychic, teacher, and author. I trained her in martial arts, where she did quite well as she learned quickly. Her classes provided me a wonderful outlet to explore my new-found sensitivities. I do now even have experience doing psychic readings for others. I had a small clientele, with mostly repeats. It was great way to gain experience doing readings. Not just to continue to understand and grow my intuition, but because there were times when someone was genuinely touched or somehow moved inside from the reading. Most said the readings were helpful, giving them a lot to think about. This has also been a helpful part of my new experience. The framework the classes provided helped me create my own "energetic framework". This personal "framework" has become part of the metaphorical foundation that I am now building upon. This is a key to always being in my most pure state of being, or "seeing" or being more attuned moment-by-moment more clearly and more consistently. In this pure state of being, no matter what the "ebb or flow", this attunement is always to intuit and be mindful to remain sensitive as I create and manifest the next part of my path in this life, one day and one moment at a time. This has been and is beneficial to be at my most effective no matter the situation or task at hand. The benefits are far reaching, including not only doing readings but other areas of life including my personal day-to-day interactions, doing presentations, when I DJ, MC, or even the writing of this book in this moment.

Things not directly related to the experience with my lady friend, yet still indirectly connected, also were "shaken loose" from these often-dark depths within. It felt like these were little energetic or emotional glitches. It would be like stepping on a thorn when you are otherwise feeling great. But this was experienced from within. I, or sometimes we, had spent time immersed in this dark vibrational energy as part of our healing... Long story for another time. As I shifted away from those dark experiences, I began seeing what can best be described as "the outlines" of karmic patterns in this life. It was like a "filmy" layer on top of the reality I am living, playing out the negative possibility of that experience. I felt these superficial reflections layered on my experience in the moment to be an alternate reality, but all dark as a reflection of my past patterns. It was like a partial dream or a remnant of a dream but with a distinctly darkened hue. This energy had stuck inside the darkest recesses of my mind for so long that it had the pungency of many years of stagnation.

To eliminate these glitchy feelings in my being was as simple as staying focused on the new path while processing these dark feelings to heal them and let them go. This process had a similar resonance of darkness to the experience with my lady friend as the catalyst that initially drew these memories and images out. It's part of the immerging synchronicity that is becoming my life (I will dive into concepts karma, light, and dark in depth in Book 2). I was feeling these thoughts coming from all parts of my life, especially from my childhood. So many memories I hadn't thought about in decades or even since early childhood were being relived in my mind. I made a point to meditate and immerse myself in those moments to relive these memories in all their nuances. It started off with some of my most ugly and difficult experiences coming through in graphic detail (This was mostly about details from my childhood. I had already recounted the memories of my time on "the streets" more times than I can remember). At times it was downright horrifying and disturbing to relive, partly because I was doing it from the perspective of when I was a small child. However, now, I can see these experiences through the current perspective of my life. It has allowed me to change the vibration of the memory in being able to make peace with it because now I see it as the person I am. After all, this too has been integral in helping me to learn and heal. That which was dark became light as I was able to make a conscious decision to make my peace. Eventually all those disturbing memories turned to some of the most precious moments of my life, not to mention, the most profound of insights and lessons I have ever had.

As I moved though my proverbial darkness, reliving and dreaming these dark memories while learning, healing, and releasing, my thoughts began to turn to many of my most precious memories. Again, so many memories I had forgotten. Dreaming of and remembering some of the most beautiful, perhaps innocent, moments of my life especially as a small child. I got to relive moments with my grandparents, all of whom passed away by the time I was 13. "Grand Dad", my dad's father, was a VP for Ford Motor Company. I was 5 when he passed away. But I can remember this big, kind smile he always wore. He was always so glad to see my brother and me. As a Ford Motors VP, he always had the nicest cars. He loved his

Lincolns! It was always fun to go for rides with Grand Dad! G-Ma, my dad's mother, passed I think when I was about 9 or maybe 10 years old. I remember she was such a sweet person. She was always singing or humming something. I remember thinking she has a brightness to her. One couldn't help but notice her always genuine endearing smile! Mimi was my mother's mother. I was 13 when she died. I remember her the best and spent the most time with her out of the grandparents. She too was the absolute sweetest, kindest, most beautiful person! I don't ever recall her being angry or upset about anything. Oh, did I mention that she was an amazing cook? Dinner at her place was always the best! She made the best salad dressing blends. She would mix different dressings, maybe add some parmesan cheese, or whatever tasted good. OMG yes, did it ever always taste good! Probably why my mom used to make some epic meals herself! The only time in my life I've ever been a card player was with Mimi. We used to play Gin Rummy mostly. She always beat me. I could never figure it out. So, I kept going back for more. She would always say, "Unlucky at cards, lucky at love." I would say she was "lucky" in both. I really cherished our time together! I never met my mother's father. He passed away before I was born. I understand he was quite the brilliant engineer. He worked for a major technological company in the early 60's. I don't recall the whole story unfortunately, but he apparently played a role in the development of what became the turbo charger in cars. There are so many of these memories that came flooding back. I made peace with my dark and now all that's left is light. It's felt so liberating!

I relived holiday and birthday moments with my parents during the time they were married. I could totally remember how I felt Christmas morning when I was 5 years old, and was even able to describe the scene around me that morning including receiving my first toy race track. I remember the day I got my first 2-wheel bicycle. I think I was 6. It was a dark green Schwinn with a black banana seat. I was so excited! I felt like I was growing up. I was very proud of the fact that I was able to learn to ride the 2-wheeler without training wheels. While there were tears of sadness and pain in my childhood, there were tears of pure joy and such an incredible happiness! It's amazing that I had so totally lost sight of some of these most wonderful times in my life. It reminded me of how it feels to truly be alive, another important piece in my healing. I feel like some of the best parts of me were when I was a child, and these best parts are reemerging because of the waking up of my child within. Life has become wondrous again!

This entire experience of reliving seemingly distant and obscure but often important and profound memories has brought such a sense of a "lightness of being", if I may coin the phrase. Even amidst the darkest, most tragic memories and all the best and lightest of memories, I have made my peace. I now see only light in my life including every dark part of my past. I feel a personal sense of freedom now, the feeling that I can be anything I want and that anything is possible! Please understand these memories are no more or less significant than those mentioned in chapter 2. The difference is I've always recalled and thought about those memories and often relived or reminisced about them whereas those above childhood memories were only recently rediscovered. Each childhood memory I shared here in this chapter had been lost for decades. It has been incredibly illuminating unto itself to experience a part of myself, as a child, that had been completely forgotten. It has brought me to a space of an inherent peace with every part myself and my life, where I discover there is a point and purpose to all of this and where I discover or rediscover something precious inside me. I never imagined until this time in my life that dreaming has always been the key to discovering or rediscovering love because of the imagination of a child or the child within. Each of us has a child within. This has been key to finding my personal light and that place of love and peace within to experience and embrace the splendors of life!

There's no question daydreaming, imagining, reliving, and coming to terms with those dark parts of me and my past were, frankly, brutal! I cried many tears, sometimes yelling out, when alone, as I purged, healed, and released these memories especially the ones where I, myself, am directly responsible for the pain and damage. I am grateful I persevered through those most difficult of old memories for them to give way to some of my life's most joyful!

There are several takeaways here... The obvious takeaway is that I have learned so much and grown in transforming as a person. I now have a sense of what aspects of my current experience resonate for me in my life now, with respect to the people and situations in my life, and what parts don't. This helps me choose my daily goals and make my decisions on the steps to take to bring them into fruition while moving forward imagining, dreaming, and creating my life in the present and future. Besides a sense of peace, I know that I have learned from these negative and difficult experiences. They are behind me now never to be repeated. I'm in a brighter place, leading me to making healthier life decisions. And, while I can't go back and change my past, what's done is done! Apologies for the bad decisions I've made and the people I've hurt in my past will change nothing. Among my fondest wishes is that the work I do now and from now on will somehow benefit these people who were harmed by me and their families in some way. This was a key part of the process of the awakening of my ability to dream again. Now, I imagine all the amazing ways life can play out and the ways I can potentially make a difference, not just for me but for everyone!

While I'm certainly far from innocent, the childlike parts of me that are emerging come from those deep recesses of my oldest, most pure being. For example, being moved perhaps to tears from a beautiful sunset by a scenic mountain view. Those unfettered and innocent parts are emerging as a part of the person I am becoming. I feel everything so much more intensely than before I fell. Yes, sometimes it can be difficult. While I feel a joy like I've not known for a long time, I also feel emotional pain or something like a heartbreak so much more deeply. I'm finding that I am "digging deep" to have the focus and balance while being so easily impacted by others and certain experiences. Make no mistake however, I wouldn't have it any other way! It's part of my inspiration in finding balance and peace!

There really is nothing love can't overcome. No matter how dark I have been in this life, no matter how rough and painful my experience may have become, no matter how much I ever just "gave up" and wanted to die, the darkest dark can find its way to light! Where there is love, it's an endless cosmos with endless possibilities, anything is possible! Expressions like "If you can dream it, you can do it" and "If you just believe, you can do anything" are clichés for a reason. They are true. How do you see your life and your reality? What are the possibilities you see when you look to your future? Do you believe you can do anything, like change or grow? The key to change through love starts with believing or more to the point knowing it's possible. Now I choose to see the most amazing possibilities all around me as I move forward on my highest path!

When considering my own "big picture" past, present, and future in continuing to grow and evolve as a person and on my path, it came down to me now taking the time to "tune-in" to recognizing and understanding of these life patterns. This includes how they apply to my life, when they began, the catalysts that set them in motion, and subsequently my choices in the midst of these experiences. This especially applies to those pivotal moments in life. This is an extension of the idea of karmic past-life patterns when looking at the perspective of multiple lives on Earth. However, just focusing on this life as Rex, I was able to recognize the pivotal, life-altering moments and path thus far. It gave me a sense of how much our decisions based on our intent and perception really do shape our reality and experience. In so doing we are always creating our reality, whether we realize it or not.

Let's consider the metaphorical "fork in the road". The experience I referenced earlier about Julie, the head cheerleader who had a crush on me when I was a sophomore in high school, is one such experience. While I understand, accept, and appreciate that everything in life has happened exactly the way it was supposed to, leading me to this point in my life and path, I recognize how differently my life might have played out if that one single experience had a different outcome. That single, seemingly innocuous experience (to go a step further, it's rooted in the negative experiences back in junior high) had lifetime ramifications. If I had made the decision to ask her out and we had connected and dated, how might my life, including potential relationships that followed including with Kim, the dance student a couple years later, have played out from there? Would I have been strong and secure enough within myself to have "come through" and pursued a relationship with Kim because of my experience with Julie? I can see the stage being set for a foundation of experience and strength within me that may have made a difference in my handling of my mother's death. Perhaps instead of it being the loss of everything I knew, including myself, I could have utilized it as motivation at that time to create something positive from my mother's death back then.

Although I am grateful for everything now, including the darkness and questionable decisions in the past that have set me free in my present, I feel it's important to explore the "what ifs" of life. If I had walked this alternative past (doubtless there is parallel reality where this is playing out), would I have still arrived at this point with the knowledge and wisdom that is now growing inside of me without having to have an NDE? But with a different set of decisions with different outcomes that would have played out a different past path, would the NDE have been needed for me "awaken"? Regardless of the path that has been playing out and the path I'm on, to coin a phrase, "it is what it is". It is all been "setting the stage" for my life and work now in this present manifesting for this future. I take this as a lesson to make different decisions when future pivotal moments come. Yes, my NDE has been a truly fantastic experience! In a way, regardless of the decisions of my past and the experiences I might have had, I'm still pretty "blown away" by this whole experience. In my life, the NDE has simply helped make it all worthwhile. I've been given a clear-cut opportunity to reinvent myself and my life. It's the chance to become everything I have always dreamed I could be and to make some dreams come true!

That singular experience as a sophomore in high school and the seemingly minor decision that I made at that time was the catalyst that catapulted a process of patterns reflecting the deep pain and darkness within me for many years moving forward. Recognizing this has put into motion a key part of my healing. Having learned and come to terms with everything from these experiences and the decisions made therein, I've since released and let them go. I'll never forget them but they are no longer an inner burden to me. This and the subsequent experiences are now a part of the best parts of me, evolving me into the person I was always meant to be and live the life I was always meant to live! When you live in this highest space of love, you feel you want to share it as often as possible! It's a big part of why I'm reaching out!

Taking responsibility and recognizing the importance of my decisions is key to navigate my path moving forward. It has been a huge part of the realization of how our decisions have such a big influence in the creation of our reality as we "walk on our respective paths". The point is to take this insight in applying it to my present, recognizing when such a powerful moment presents itself again. And it will present itself again (this is true of all of us). I can feel it! Another big shift and transformation are coming. However, this time, I can be sure to do my part in seizing opportunities as presented, especially potentially life changing opportunities! I am confident that I won't have to miss them again, only to chalk it up to a lesson I should already have learned. Not ever again!! "Carpe Diem!!" Take care of the present and the future will take care of itself. Perhaps, most importantly, there have been many powerful insights with the chance for significant growth. I have/am absolutely taking full advantage. For the first time in my life I am truly comfortable in saying, "I love myself, I love my life, I simply love...!"

I find that I'm quite comfortable and clear to myself regarding, at the very least, my own personal boundaries in trusting in myself and my intuition, knowing what supports what's best for me, what's best for all of those with whom I am sharing experience, and what supports my overall path. Conversely, if I feel like I'm not a positive in someone's life, if my presence is somehow negative despite the love in my heart and my best intentions, I'll remove myself. Again, love does what is best for a person and/or situation in bringing it to its highest state of fulfillment and contentment... sometimes including letting go.

I'm not sure that I can pick just one blessing that sticks out over any others. Since the NDE, there have been so many wonders. But among my favorites is the band, "Quantum Beings of the Miraculous". This has been a most "miraculous" and most unexpected part of my experience. There's one small detail about this band... I'm actually in it. It truly is a gift! And what an incredible gift! While I spent years in event promotion and artist development (I worked with lots of great bands/artists), I never thought I would be in a band. I'm a DJ. I have played with live musicians like percussionists, a sax player, keyboard player, and a few others. However, that's a far cry from playing with five other people in a band. Yes, I DJ in the band. I drop beats, riffs, and samples depending on the song. But the best part of this experience is that I am becoming a musician. I have been quite diligently practicing hand-drumming. I mostly play the congas. I have played djembe's, bongos, and a few other drums. I currently play drums on about a half-dozen songs with Quantum Beings and will be playing on more as we are always writing new songs. All my bandmates, including our drummer Canine mentioned earlier, are talented multi-instrumentalists. It means a lot to me that they support me and help me to learn! We have written songs that have come from ideas I have presented to the band. I appreciate that they are always open to my ideas considering I have a small fraction of their experience and musical knowledge...I'm excited to say it's made for some great songs that have been performed many times! Whether a small piece of atmosphere in a song or key element of a song, this whole song writing and performing thing has been an incredible experience in connection and synergy! What an amazing gift and blessing this has been!

Since 2014, Quantum Beings has been playing shows and we've released an album. The album is called "Through the Gates". A second is coming called "Regents of the Mystics". While we play clubs, we have thus far been more of a festival band. These are festivals that are part of the "Burning Man" culture around Colorado, New Mexico, and San Diego. I've met a lot of wonderful people and shared the stage with many talented artists. Quantum Beings will be recording our second album soon. We have enough music to do a couple more albums. The creative process flows easily for us. It's so much fun!

I feel blessed to be walking a path where I have had the opportunity to touch others and be touched. While this book has been years in the making, I have been given the opportunities to present my story and many of the lessons. I have dreamed of being a musician since I was a child. But, like many children, I've also dreamed of being a filmmaker and I did also imagine being an author. While all these parts of my life are growing and evolving, given the work I've done at this point, I have become a musician, filmmaker, and speaker. I just mentioned my band and the drumming. As of the release of this book, I am an author. I am currently a member of the Denver Open Media, where I have the opportunity to learn about the entire production process both in studio and on location. All of their gear is "state of the art". I have produced and hosted a series of shows called, "The New Revolution". The goal of the show is to interview many different people, old and young, from many walks of life. The goal is to learn about who they are, what they believe, what love is to them, their dreams, and ways we may take steps towards creating peace in the world for everyone. I plan to take this show all over the world. I've spent several years doing public speaking on subjects related to or inspired by my NDE.

Some parts of my pre-NDE life are still a part of me. I am still a DJ. I love it as much now as when I was just first starting out! Martial arts, or in particular Kun Tao Silat, is still and always will be prevalent in my life. This Kun Tao Silat training is part of my foundation, balance and personal grounding. There are so many different dynamics happening all at once in my life in the present. I see more and more things synchronizing or coming together. Not just through the space of the now, but through time. It's been a process with the purging and healing of my memories, to find peace in my present, to grow on my path being the best person I can be for my future. All these seemingly different parts of my life are coming together in a symphony of melodies and harmonies. It's such beautiful music!

This time since my NDE has been so powerful in so many ways! While I focus to stay mindful of being in my loving space, the experience has its proverbial "ebbs and flows", as with most of us. I have been deeply touched by many people and the experiences we have shared. I have watched those I care about on their respective paths. Some are stuck in struggles that they can't, in the moment, seem to find their way out of. I see what they can do to help themselves, but I know it will fall on "deaf ears" if I say or do anything that could help. Sometimes it's hard to watch someone you care about in that struggle. Still others have amazed and humbled me with their wonderful beauty of being! I always appreciate how much I have learned through these experiences with these people with whom I have shared experience. For all the ugliness of the world, there is so much more beauty and wonder to be experienced! This is where it feels right to focus my energy. Not that I'm blocking out the negative but rather I don't want to feed the negative with worry, doubt, sympathy (I believe in empathy), anger, self-preservation, or any such fear-based experience. I will focus on feeding the positive love-based experience. That starts with teaching people that there are ways through everything, no matter how difficult. While I take every opportunity to observe and learn in hearing what others have to say, I find I learn just as much when I'm presenting or teaching. This is another example of seizing opportunities to grow in being the person I always dreamed I could be!

In the years since my NDE, I feel like I have been slowly coming back into my true self and the child within. The thoughts, ideas, epiphanies, feelings I have shared in this book are the result of a more deeply visual imagination and as such more deeply vivid dreaming. All of this has come from that most childlike, most innocent, and yes, most vulnerable, most purely real parts of me. Starting with those early moments while in the hospital after falling I could feel something was different, despite how bad it all looked initially. Aside from the head injury issues, while I had the occasional "down" moment, I was never actually worried. I was generally in a positive mind set, especially following my hospital stay. Somehow, it would take time but I knew it would all work out. At the time, I felt like I would come through this. I knew then as I know now that this singular moment in having a near-death experience was the most powerful and impactful moment of my life. Talk about a pivotal life-altering "fork in the road". This NDE has been the experience that gave me the chance to choose a completely different path. A path that supports the best of changes in me and my ability to impact the world, that of my highest path!

The realization that something incredible happened while near-death began when I was in the hospital. Shortly after that, the epiphanies started. I became increasingly curious about this concept of near-death experience.   After being released from the hospital, I started studying other people's NDE's online. Eventually, a main doctor who oversaw my care from the beginning confirmed that he would consider what I experienced to be a near-death experience. As I realized and came to accept that what happened was a bona fide NDE, I was encouraged to explore the thoughts and feelings that were pouring in. This was a choice in putting this potentially tragic experience into perspective. That could have become the worst or the best event in my life. This could have fueled my anger and self-loathing (after all I almost died falling out of a tree), but I chose to let it inspire! Now I dream about manifesting dreams into the experience or simply, making dreams come true. Not just for me but for everyone! How about we do this together? We are stronger together than alone. How do we bridge the gaps that divide us? How do we end war and hunger? How do we make sure all have their most basic needs (food, medicine, education...) met no matter what? How do we inspire people to be the best they can be in making their dreams come true? What steps do we take or what is the process? I believe we can solve this together!

I can't seem to get enough of the dreams of the experiential consciousness itself - the divine, gravity, connectivity, soul experience, and so much more that I am discovering as I expand into this source consciousness. I have realized that it's not just about my individual experience but simply, the experience itself. Since falling in 2011, I really do have the sense of "being in a dream within a dream" as Poe so eloquently expressed. But then I realize, no matter how you look at your experience, no matter how simplistic or complex, it's all just different aspects of the same dream, the divine dream!

7

The World Experience: Awakening

So often, our life decisions are based on our personal life environment throughout the course of a life. We can get into a pattern of responding to the stimuli around us, letting that pattern be the guide or teacher. This can influence crucial decisions in our life, even in the belief that we are subject to the happenstance of a day. Even the belief of having no control over the course of your life is still a decision that, though we may not realize it, guides what happens and the outcomes through our perception of having no control or influence. We often individually and collectively believe that we are basically "products of our environment" or "victims of circumstance". As such, we make decisions based on this view of reality where options, especially positive options, are limited or nonexistent.

Many of us get caught up in the ego part of ourselves, being subject to our most primal desires as a result of being always on the edge of "fight or flight". This thought pattern reinforces the belief that we are alone and separated. We've heard the expression, "We're born alone, and we die alone." It's a fairly common perception in the Western world. In that space, we don't have a conscious inclination to make the best decision for ourselves and those around us. Many people struggle to make positive and life supporting decisions for themselves individually, let alone considering what's best for someone else or a situation as a whole. We can act selfishly as the result of human ego with the wantings and cravings or obsessions and infatuations that can emerge from it. These cravings of infatuation and obsession that feed the primal urges are not out of love but out of self-centeredness, selfishness, and self-gratification. This can include money, sex, intoxication, and territorial and personal domination among many other things based just in materialism and the ego. This behavior not only feeds the moment, but it becomes an overwhelming physical sensory experience that can unto itself be addicting. It's generally on the most superficial levels, thought the damage can be soul deep.

This experience is like standing on a beach looking out over the ocean. As one peers into the distance, it seems to go off forever. We can't see the other side. We may observe clouds above and maybe a brightly shining sun or, if at night, the moon and a sky full of stars. We may see the waves crashing into shore. If we look closely, we may see waves and ripples in those waves within the main wave moving towards shore. In that moment, there is so much to "take in" and experience while looking out over the ocean. But for all of its vastness and detail, it still doesn't begin to come close to that which exists beneath the ocean's surface and beyond the sun and stars above. We must not only realize but begin to imagine how much more there is from within and without all of us. This is how we will understand who and what we really are and what this whole grand experience really is. What we perceive to be real and how we choose to apply this in our lives is limited only by the bounds of the imagination, not the bounds of our environment and society.

The capacity exists to see ourselves from within from a sub-conscious or, if I may, a sub-atomic state of mind. It happens when one can come to see and intuit within oneself through self-actualization. As we individually actualize our deepest existence and accept what it is at the core of our being, it becomes natural to carry that out accordingly, including the natural inclination to share love and experience with others. This is a truth of what one is meant to be versus what our outward self-serving desire tells us. We won't always get what we wish, especially those cravings based on our more physical desires, our physical brain's conscious thought, and a superficially-based hope especially based in the "me" perspective of "I want". However, the expression mentioned earlier "be careful what you wish for, you just might get it" sometimes applies. It's an affirmation that perhaps you aren't yet in the space where your wishes align and resonate with your "higher self". The true reality may be different in how it appears in the superficially-based reality given one's potential inclination to disconnect from that deeper part of us based on the core truth from the core source or spirit in favor of physical ego-based gratification.

The perception of our personal truth about our place in this world or on our path has everything to do with the current moment in our personal space/time. This can impact the perspective of where one believes one is at a particular moment in space/time or moment in one's life versus where one could or potentially should be. How it plays out, often in the long term, reflects our deepest being or soul. This deepest being harbors the core truths we all carry at the source of consciousness. Eventually, what is meant for us based on that deepest place from within our being is what will always come through in the long run. This is different for every one of us as each experience is unique. If you're living "out of tune" or "out-of-phase" with your deeper self and reality, it may make for some difficult and challenging life experiences and patterns. You might find yourself feeling distracted, lost, and empty. Often times, this may involve some difficult life experiences to find and evolve into that deeper unconscious soul space. Sometimes these are the most difficult and traumatic experiences, the kind that can potentially break a person. But these can also build up a person to indomitable levels of strength and the wisdom of divinity and consciousness in a quest for true personal understanding. We must make the decision! We typically have to dig very deep inside to find the strength and means to persevere through these most challenging of experiences. What can come out when digging to the depths of true being can be quite stupendous. Though often a long, arduous process, doing this will bring about a general deeper understanding of the self, those around you, and even an understanding of what the divine, consciousness, and existence are and mean to you. The more we do this the more we move into a life we have dreamed about instead of simply being subject to an experience that takes you "off path", perhaps for another life lesson. This is opening one's heart and exploring ultimate truth as revealed to oneself.

What would it take to create a worldwide epiphany toward a worldwide raising of consciousness? Possibly the confirmation of intelligent life outside the Earth may propel a rapid shift in our collective conscious perspective. Perhaps a great disaster or some form of shared worldwide hardship would draw out our empathy and interpersonal connection. There was a great amount of speculation regarding the symbolism of December 21st, 2012. Some suggested it was the "end of days" here on Earth, with possibly catastrophic worldwide disasters, because the Mayan calendar, as some believed, forecasted a major event on this date. But what was it the end of? Still others say it's was a changing of "ages" - a kind of "resetting" of the calendar. According to Mayan lore, this is when the 13th baktun (age) finished and the 14th began, suggesting some kind of paradigm shift. In Hindu philosophy, there is the belief of the changing of ages from Kali Yuga to

Satya Yuga. In some Western astrology, we are moving from the "age of Pisces" to the "age of Aquarius". Each purports us to be in the process of shifting now. Generally, the belief with each refers to moving from a violent, materialist, fear-based paradigm to a more peaceful, loving one. This may be symbolic of the many people who are raising their own consciousness around the world. It's the start of a worldwide raising of consciousness. I can see many searching for the core truths more now than anytime I can remember in my life. And it's people of all types and ages. I hear more and more so many deeper truths spoken by many people. Even on social forums, where substance can sometimes be lacking, I see glimmers of this deeper understanding popping up in a post or meme, some advice given as a result of a post, or maybe the sharing of an experience in the mountains or out on the ocean or with someone close. I hold out hope that we as a people can grow without the need for major disasters in order for us to feel the kind of empathy for one another to want to help and not hurt, the kind of empathy where you feel the inherent love that is natural between us. You can't feel that love for someone and not want to help and protect them. It may take something catastrophic, deeply humbling and beautiful, or a profound discovery for us to experience a collective Earth-wide coming together through empathy and love. That's a big "time will tell".

I often wonder what will happen if we continue to neglect ourselves and our planet. How long can it all last with the way things are going in the world? The Earth is changing fast! There are NO new lessons to be learned from our wars, famine, hunger, and all the hardship in our world. We've pretty much "been there done that" many times over. We've brought it upon ourselves. The more we as a people damage our planet, the more we have to face our responsibility and role in that too. We kill, people grieve, and many lives are ruined. This is a road too often traveled by the human race. We know it well. We, as the most intelligent most dominant species on the planet, must take responsibility for our decisions and actions throughout history, the world today, and the reality we have created as a result of our collective self-centeredness, fear, anger, judgment, selfishness, ignorance and obliviousness. We, as a race, have been guilty of negligence and malevolence to ourselves, each other, our society and our planet. We are now even turning the space around our planet into a junkyard.

If we ever hope to have the chance to find our collective peace and be a benefit to planet Earth, much must change. What will be our legacy in the annals of space/time? Will it be that the most advanced and intelligent species to ever inhabit this planet could be amongst the shortest lived as a result of our own undoing? Or will we, as the human race, finally collectively "wake up," coming together as one people, in one world, in one universe, and one consciousness? Will we "wake up" to see the divinity within us all in the core source of consciousness out to the cosmos and back to the source consciousness, God? Will we "wake up" to see ourselves make our way to the stars in a long and productive existence evolving to fulfill our deepest potential? We are in complete control of our destiny as a people and a collective worldwide consciousness, however it plays out. In the "here and now", we can't change the past, but only learn from it. Nevertheless, we have our free will and the means to choose to create virtually anything we wish for the entire world moving forward. Let's create peace!

Change and growth have to start with each individual person if we are to be strong and grow as a whole. There is the potential for everyone, regardless of who you are or where you call home, to see past the distractions that dominate in our lives and the world. There is the potential for everyone to see that we, the Earth, and the heavens beyond are all one while discovering your personal vision and mission in life!

An argument can be made that one day many aspects of

science and spirituality/metaphysics will evolve to the point of becoming one. It seems a natural progression to advancements in these fields and our collective growth over time, though there is still much for us to learn. Science tells us that there is far, far more we have to learn than what we currently know. However, we do have many resources from which to draw for information. In seeking enlightenment, we can draw from our own history, modern science, religion/philosophy, each other, and so many other amazing things available to us in our own lives. Throughout history, there have been those great teachers of humanity who have hoped to guide us. We should, at the least, give true consideration to gain insight from any such individual who has in the past or will in the future contribute to the evolution of knowledge and wisdom of both science and spirituality with the hope of helping to expand minds.

Can you imagine a round table discussion with people like Jesus Christ, Muhammad, Lao Tzu, Siddhartha Gautama (the first Buddha), Krishna, Kuan Yin, Sitting Bull, Haile Selassie, Zoroaster (Zarathustra), Confucius, and Bahá'u'lláh (among others)? Do you think they would be arguing and judging each other about whose path to God is right or wrong? I'm inclined to believe that they would all share an immense love and special respect for one another. There would doubtless be a sharing of incredible wisdom without ego. But then, they may just simply enjoy each other's company and share some genuine laughs. They would certainly respect and understand that each represents reality, love, life, the divine from different parts of the world and different points in time and therefore with different expressions and experiences. On the surface, they appear quite different. But they are more alike than different, as we all are. Each teacher/ prophet and the religions they represent share the ideals of love, virtue, and peace as the foundations of their respective philosophies and beliefs. Some of the methods and ways of explaining may seem to differ on the surface, but the underlying message is the same. It's about love!

In our modern world, we have the benefit of science. It has made a small dent in our tangible understanding of our nature, our environment, and the universe, both micro and macro. Science may be at the initial stages in explaining the mysteries regarding consciousness and God. Multiple fields of study such as quantum theory, astrophysics, cosmology, and other emerging fields of science are seeking to find answers regarding the innermost and outermost aspects of our universe and existence. There are many top scientists, past and present, including Albert Einstein and Max Planck, who believed or do believe in ideals of God and divinity. Both Einstein and Planck, as one might expect, had many interesting and thought-provoking insights on God. Certain modern-day scientists like Stuart Hameroff (anesthesiologist, quantum theorist) and Sir Roger Penrose (award winning mathematical physicist) have a working theory called Orchestrated Objective Reduction. This theory links quantum states in the human brain with consciousness. Of course, it's a subject of great debate in the scientific community. But it is an example of science starting to converge with the spiritual. It would be amazing to be alive at a time when science and spirituality finally catch up to each other and do truly converge into one field of study. The resulting knowledge would be spectacular and incredibly transformational for the entire planet. Perhaps that can play a key role in the worldwide epiphany for which many are awaiting??

For that wisdom which currently eludes science, we have our most important tool for enlightenment, ourselves! We have an infinite capacity for empathy, intuition, imagination, and love. As mentioned earlier these are all key qualities our evolution and true nature as people. Each quality is quite specific to the evolutionary process. It helps us to resonate with and see truths that science can't yet explain. How often do most people "get a feeling" about something, especially something that is not currently provable, but yet feels right? Or perhaps a feeling about something tangible that requires time to be revealed? For example, you have a job interview. Even though you know the prospective company is still going to interview for another 2+ weeks, you leave feeling like or even knowing you will be offered the job. After a couple of weeks, you get that phone call with a job offer. There was no tangible proof or indication at the time of the interview that you would get the job. But something simply resonated with it and turned out to be right. Granted, some people are better at this than others, but the point is you may have such a feeling, something that resonates, about how you feel or believe about any number of areas like that of God, spirituality, and metaphysics. Sometimes we just "know" something. It simply feels like truth. You may not be able to prove or disprove it but you know somehow it is right! Whether it's something tangible and "down to Earth" or something more esoteric beyond current-day science, this feeling stems from your source consciousness or divine being. It proves to be personal truth for you. With time, practice, and the belief I learned/still learning to do it, I have learned to trust in my feelings or my intuition. Yes, it is a practice. Intuition is a reflection of the core conscious vibration at the source of us all, the soul. It is perhaps our most powerful guide. This may manifest with angels, passed loved ones, and/or various forms of "spirit guides" as per one's personal beliefs and experience.

There seems to be a common ground among many people these days about these core truths that resonate. These expressions come across all cultural, racial, religious, sexual, and political boundaries. I find more and more that many people share these certain deeper truths. However, there are many ways to explain and express such ideals. As I get to know both spiritual and scientific people more, I have enjoyed the many wonderful ways these truths can be spoken. I'm not sure there's a particularly large gap between what the Vedas, native peoples, or others were saying hundreds, if not thousands of years ago, and what people like Planck and Einstein, or Nassim Haramein, Amit Goswami, or Jonathan Hagelin, modern day theoretic physicists, have said about consciousness. I hear many varying forms of these trains of thought in varying degrees from many people around me. These truths are starting to "come to life" in society regardless of religion, race, etc. A shift is happening!

Often language falls short of doing justice to expressing such thoughts and ideals. Even though, in theory, words have a specific definition as can be found in any dictionary, there are still subtle variations in the interpretations of those definitions for each of us. Ultimately, the choices of words used to describe the same thing may vary. I have been in many conversations, especially about these deeper more esoteric subjects, or even having a healthy debate over a particular topic, only to eventually realize that the person I'm conversing with and I are saying the same basic thing. As I have said, I feel underneath the surface we are more alike than different.

With all of the qualities that encapsulate the divine or God, becoming one with this source spirit and evolving consciousness is a perfectly natural process for each of us. I'm not suggesting it will be an easy process, but that it is perfectly natural sometimes despite appearances. This makes getting through those "ups and downs" easier because the realization helps to provide a sense of purpose and guidance. This is inherent by our own design, the design of creation, and by the nature of the divine. But evolving vibration to resonate in love must be done with an open heart, trust with an unwavering belief it's all happening "for the best". You can't find your vision of God or truly find yourself without love. Look deep inside yourself right down to the source of consciousness and pure being and rediscover that innocent childlike wonder bringing outward the love from deep within. With it, experience the splendor, beauty, and that ultimate fulfillment that is the potential for our lives, the world, and the Earth. Know this singular divine being - you - for yourself. You have everything you need! Every time you look at yourself, a loved one, a friend, the family pet, or any living being, you see God. Every person, animal, lake, ocean, plain, forest, mountain peak, cloud in the sky, or star above is the experience of God. Every breath you take, every scent that touches your nose, every sound that fills your ears, and all that touches your skin is the sensation of God. Every thought, idea, or feeling from the purist love and state of absolute contentment to the harshest of feelings and desire is to feel the emotion of God. To see your own vision of the divine is to know God. Through it all, to just simply be... with love... is to wake up and realize you are one with yourself, all people, the Earth, the universe, and one in the same with God! We are a living, breathing experience of the divine dream!

8

Final Thoughts for Now...

My NDE helped to propel an awakening to "see" like I never have before! I am grateful for such a powerful experience! It's a catalyst to manifesting the ongoing fulfillment of life dreams. I feel blessed! But yes, I must still make the decision to "do my part" in the moment. However, I'm not sure most would want to go through such a painful and difficult process, like an NDE, toward their awakening. Thankfully you do not have to. To be perfectly clear, **you don't have to have an NDE to experience a profound personal awakening! There are many paths to enlightenment. This information is within us and around us all!**

My time with drug addiction and being on the streets was probably the wildest most careless time of my life. I did some careless things while in Colorado Springs but the time on the streets in Denver were the wildest. I was completely reckless! Of course, that's the time when I probably did the most damage to others and to myself. A lot of people got hurt including me. I take full responsibility for my decisions and actions. That was all a long time ago now. At this point, perhaps there are those, like me, who have moved on in their lives. They may not think about these past events anymore because it is behind them. Perhaps they have found forgiveness. Perhaps they too have learned what they have needed to learn and have evolved and moved on. But then again, perhaps not. Maybe some wound up in jail or even dead. For those that have moved on, I hope these individuals have grown and maybe gotten married and have families or are just living a happy, abundant life!

I can't change the past but I can affect the present and help change the future. As I have experienced, there are a handful of people who have not forgiven me for certain actions from my past. I do understand and take no offense. I've resolved myself to the feeling that since I can't change or fix some the damage to others in the past, perhaps I can manifest the creation of something positive for all people. This especially includes those who I have wronged or hurt and especially those who have may still not be able to forgive me. Even if they don't think I deserve forgiveness, I still hope they can find it in their hearts to forgive and let go even just for their own sake. It's so internally heavy, painful, and negative to carry such burdens. Some carry them for so long they forget they are there. But when the day comes to let them go, it never ceases to amaze how much "lighter" people always say they feel. I hope I can help those and all people set free all their burdens when they believe they are ready. That, of course is the key - being ready.

Now I am free to experience giving and receiving all the love and beauty of life with all my heart! While the most difficult and challenging of experiences, I'm thankful for what truly is has been the most profound and transformational event in my whole life! While I certainly wouldn't want to do it again, I am nonetheless immensely thankful for this experience! It has inspired me to change my life in ways I couldn't have at one time thought possible. I'm glad I wasn't given a choice about crossing over and moving on from this life because I would have gone. Now, I have a second chance to live life with love and make dreams come true! This includes planting the seeds of positive change in the world! That is my greatest dream! I may not be able to change the past where once I caused pain but I can look to a future where I can help heal pain and make the world a better place for everyone!

In realizing our inherent connection to each other, the Earth, and the Universe, we can begin to realize how hurting another person is the same as hurting ourselves. It's compromising to our vibration and a poison to our soul. Such a person may ultimately become hardened as a result. Once a person has begun a path of causing damage or hurt to others, it just gets easier as the person becomes harder and colder. But to be able to see all the ways we a connected, it becomes increasingly difficult to hurt another because we empathize and feel that they are somehow a part of us. We may feel each other's feelings. We can feel when others are happy, sad, content, or hurt. We know if we have disappointed or hurt someone in the way that we can tell when we have touched someone in a beautiful way.

We, as people, can be so naturally protective and readily willing to help the ones closest to us. But why not everyone? After all, we are all related. Is it only instinctive for a small percentage of people to have that same sense of loving protectiveness and helpfulness toward all life and our planet? We live in a world that is intentioned and designed for division and the illusion of separation. There are many things in society that are designed to promote isolation and separation, exacerbating the feeling of being alone, desperate, or perhaps just plain miserable. Even groups of people can feel isolated and alone in fighting for a cause. Such groups may believe the "us against the world" paradigm. Society is also designed to promote competition in just about every facet of life. Competition in sports is one thing. I'm all in favor of sports. I believe they are an important part of our current-day society. But competition in life is sometimes vicious and leaves deep personal damage. It can become predatory. Even when it's "just business", it can have a devastating impact on those involved.

On the one hand, it brings out a massive ego with a proclivity for excessive materialism. In many, it will bring out a sense of self-centeredness and entitlement. It's the illusion of the "haves and have nots" that can bring out a bully mentality. These experiences leave many people destitute and feeling broken inside especially being on the "wrong end of business". Lives can be ruined to the point of putting someone out on the street without a home and even suicidal. It's not just about any one of us, but all of us! Whether we like it or not, believe it or not, the evidence whether, esoteric, scientific, social, financial, or political, is everywhere. We are and everything is connected! We are one people in one world! We are ALL in this together!

Imagine living in a world where love, compassion and virtue are the norm. Imagine a world where everyone takes care of themselves, each other, and the planet. That is a mentality and way of life that "goes without saying" to help and nurture others when the opportunity presents itself. Imagine a world where a person grows from birth in finding his or her talents and passions and is supported in that highest path. Imagine every man, woman, and child having the means and ability to have a productive, abundant, fulfilling, and loving life. Imagine this has been the way of life on Earth over many generations. In a world where everyone is fully supported in becoming almost anything, I believe the slackerism we see in society today would all but disappear. Everyone would have the freedom to be the best person they can be in who and what they are and what they choose! It would be the freedom to live their dreams in love and abundance. What would such a world be like? Peaceful, for starters. The advancements in science and spirituality and the prospective merger would be amazing in such a world of deeper understanding, cooperation, and growth! But such a world happens when we are all accepting, encouraging, caring, and compassionate towards each other and everybody. Beauty in life would be as paramount in all aspects of society as ugliness seems to be today. Yet despite the ugly side of life being thrown at us from the media and other sources, beauty in life is still far more abundant! It is both inside of us and all around us! Here's to growing worldwide abundance! Here's to everyone living their dream or learning to take steps to living their dream! The more of us living the life of our dreams, the closer we come to living in the world of our dreams! Let's keep spreading the love... and may all of our dreams come true!

To put it mildly, "Holy moly, this life has been quite the ride so far!" I think of comedian Bill Hicks and his "life is a ride" bit. It's funny and quite poignant! For all the awesomeness in my life now, I can only imagine and dream of a future that continues to grow in love! Gravity has certainly asserted itself in my life and my dreams. Strangely I feel gravity has given me something special that goes beyond the fall or NDE and will be a part of me moving forward. I do have a certain gratitude for gravity! It is a key to the inspiration of my imagination. I'm dreaming with the excitement and wonder of a child. I can't wait to see what's come for me, you, and yes, the world!

Thank you for taking some time with my story! I sincerely do hope some part of my story can help you with some part of yours! Thank you to all the people throughout my entire life who have been a part of my experience whether as a casual passing incident, the lifelong experience, or something in-between! You are all part of me as I am with you!

Here's to living the life of our dreams, here's to abundance, and here's to love! To mother Earth and everyone in the whole world, **I love you!!**